PREACHING GOD'S WORD ON SUNDAY

To the memory of
Marie McAteer
1916-1996

Desmond Knowles

Preaching God's Word on Sunday

HOMILIES AND PRAYER OF THE FAITHFUL
FOR YEAR C OF THE THREE-YEAR CYCLE

the columba press

First published in 2006 by
the columba press
55A Spruce Avenue, Stillorgan Industrial Park,
Blackrock, Co Dublin

Cover by Bill Bolger
Origination by The Columba Press
Printed in Ireland by ColourBooks Ltd, Dublin

ISBN 1 85607 547 8

Copyright © 2006, Desmond Knowles

Table of Contents

Acknowledgments

A book like this would not be possible without the help and support of several people. Many thanks to those good friends who have given generously of their time in proof-reading these homilies as well as those who offered honest and valuable criticism. I am deeply indebted to Celine McAteer who composed the Prayer of the Faithful, which flows directly from the theme of the particular Sunday homily.

Introduction

St Francis of Assisi instructed his followers to 'Preach always, sometimes with words', indicating the power of good example, which is within everyone's reach. However, priests and deacons are mandated to preach 'with words' and in this book I have been mindful of the obligation to share 'the unsearchable riches of Christ' (Ephesians 3:8). Preaching is both a privileged and a humbling activity requiring prayerful and careful preparation. One of the greatest challenges to the preacher throughout his years of ministry is to take what he knows from his study of theology and express it in a language that can be understood by his congregation. Its content must be something that awakens a living faith in worshippers so that they may turn their minds and hearts towards God and be renewed in their commitment to Christ's call to discipleship. Jesus used language that evoked images and appealed to the imagination. So should we. By connecting the 'Good News' of the gospel with the real-life concerns of the congregation, the preacher is giving his listeners encouragement in their daily lives. The homilies contained in this book are the result of my preaching experience over a period of seven years as an emigrant chaplain in Paris and five years as a parish priest in Ireland. A single theme has been chosen for each homily since the preacher generally has around seven minutes at his disposal. My hope is that this collection of homilies may provide a stimulus for thought and be of some help in the understanding of the faith and in the search for God.

1st Sunday of Advent
First Reading: Jeremiah 33:14-16;
Second Reading: 1 Thess 3:12-4:2; Gospel: Luke 21:25-28, 34-36

We have often heard it said that if something is worth doing it is worth doing well. When a social event, like a wedding or anniversary, is planned, much preparation is needed. Guest lists are drawn up, invitations sent out and your own experience will testify to a hundred and one other jobs that have to be done. It is not all hardship as there is an element of joy and anticipation in the waiting and that's how it is with Advent. Each year as the light of the day diminishes, the season of Advent makes its gentle way into our churches. It marks the beginning of a month long liturgical season during which the church asks us to awaken our spiritual selves by making the necessary preparations for the coming of Jesus Christ into our world. Aside from the incessant moaning and groaning about the aggressive commercialism of the period, Christmas is an important event in the Christian calendar. Advent provides us with an opportunity to get a proper perspective on what the festival is really about. It helps us to avoid the boredom that seems to come from the actual celebration of a Christ-less Christmas. Ours is a culture of artificially created longings. So often, at this time of year, our senses are dulled and distracted from what is really important, by the great shopping spree. We get sucked into the fast and furious craze of buying bigger and better presents. In the process we forget about making our lives worthy places where the Lord can dwell.

If Christmas is to have a religious meaning, the four weeks of Advent are about putting our lives in order by preparing a place in our hearts for the best news ever proclaimed, the story of God's unbounded love for us. It is a time set aside for reflection on the threefold coming of Christ into our world. We miss the whole point of celebrating the arrival of Jesus into our midst at Bethlehem if we fail to see that the child born in a manger will come again as judge and redeemer on the last day to bring history to a glorious conclusion. It is for this that we pray at Mass when we recite together, 'As we wait in joyful hope for the coming of our Saviour Jesus Christ.'

Waiting is something we have all experienced and it is part of our way of life. We have all known the frustration of waiting in a traffic jam when we are in a hurry, the anxious waiting for the outcome of a hospital appointment or for the result of an exam. Nevertheless, the spirit of Advent, waiting and hoping for something better to happen, touches the agonies and longings of every human heart. We witness this in lives turned upside down by the unexpected death of a loved one, in the loss of employment or when a partner decides to walk out on a marriage. Lives, which only yesterday were so orderly and minutely planned, are suddenly faced with insecurity knocking at the door. For many the end of the world talked about in today's gospel is not a future fantasy but an unhappy element of daily experience. When life is rocked to its foundations and despair is setting in, Advent encourages us to hold on and keep hoping. It assures us that there is more to our worth than what we look like, where we live and the car we drive. God is at work and misery, disappointment and death do not have the last word. Whatever happens, it should comfort us to remember that Christ chose to come among us and begin his mission on earth in the vulnerable state of a newborn baby, in the humble surroundings of a stable.

The central and most important preparation we can make during Advent is prayer, which is loving attentiveness to God. Taking time to pray involves setting aside some part of each day to make a place for God. It means closing the door to distractions and making space in a busy schedule where we can be alone, have silence and quiet time in sacred stillness.

Prayer nourishes our relationship with the Lord by making us aware of the Divine Presence in our lives. When we pray we delve below the surface happenings of our days and nights and we discover God who dwells in our depths. Advent invites us to make our lives ready for the Lord who is to come.

Prayer of the Faithful

As we begin the new Church year, we pray to God our Father to help us prepare for the coming of the Lord into our world and into our lives.

1. We pray that the church may continue to shine as a beacon of light drawing all people towards Christ and his kingdom.
   Lord, hear us.

2. That, as a community, we may not fail to recognise the coming of Christ in those we meet in the course of our day.
   Lord, hear us.

3. For families divided by misunderstanding or mistrust, that they may experience a renewal of love and peace with each other.
   Lord, hear us.

4. We pray for the sick, those who are hospitalised and those who have no one to care for them – may they experience God's healing presence.
   Lord, hear us.

5. We pray for those who have died and for those who have lost their loved ones. Comfort them in their need.
   Lord, hear us.

God our Father, grant that this Advent season may draw us more closely to your Son, Jesus. Give us the strength to know your ways and to walk in your footsteps. We make our prayer through Christ, our Lord. Amen.

2nd Sunday of Advent
First Reading: Baruch 5:1-9;
Second Reading: Philippians 1:3-6, 8-11; Gospel: Luke 3:1-6

When the outlook is bleak and everything is doom and gloom it is surprising how a little bit of good news can change the situation. We could say that sadness was the prevailing mood of the Israelites during the exile in Babylon when the prophet Baruch sounded a note of joy telling them that God had not forgotten his people. Good times are about to come again, so they are to cheer up, put on their good clothes, pack their bags and prepare for the journey home, back to Jerusalem. Advent is about being a wanderer, lost in exile and then realising the importance of coming home to God. It is a solemn season of quiet, in the darkness of the year, for contemplating the light of the Christ-child. In order to do this we need to tune in and create space for prayerful reflection on the Nativity and set aside something of the world's demands. This is a message with great relevance for our times when the frantic hustle and bustle of the modern secular Christmas leaves precious little time for dwelling on things spiritual. It was a thought summed up very well in the short poem of Thomas Merton – 'Into this world, this demented inn, in which there was no room for him at all, Christ came uninvited.'

We may well ask how should we prepare ourselves for the coming of Christ so that he may join us at our festive table. Our preparations for Christmas somewhat miss the mark if there is nothing more to the generous giving than exchanging bigger and better presents with our friends. If we merely look after our friends, we may well be observing social niceties but what about the message of Advent, which is stated in the gospel line, 'All mankind shall see the salvation of God'? This means that there are to be no outsiders. The hungry, the homeless and everyone on the margins of society are to be included. We are called to bring the light of salvation to them through our healing words and acts of kindness. In order to discover Christ, we need to rid ourselves of all the tinsel trappings, open our door to the poor and have time for the neglected. We do not want to be numbered among those who have no space in their hearts or in their home for the redeeming Christ.

Within the wilderness of our human sinfulness the voice of John the Baptist speaks an Advent message of repentance. It is an invitation to take time out and let the spirit of God get to work in our lives in order to make a pathway through all that hinders us from growing in his love. For this to happen, only one thing is necessary and that is that we accept his call to repentance. Repentance is not just a mild regret for the wrongs of the past but a longing for a change of heart and a turning away from the attitudes that constantly bring us back to a repetition of the same old failings. Serious reflection is needed on what improvements we must make in our lives. What we long for, hope for and wait for this Advent may mean a radical change of lifestyle. Change seems so difficult and unsettling because leaving the comfortable and the familiar can make us feel fearful, threatened and uneasy. All this may seem beyond our reach, but when the Spirit of God is at work, hearts of stone can be turned into hearts of flesh. The insurmountable barriers that block our way are as nothing to the forgiveness of the God who comes among us in the person of Christ. He will never disappoint and what he offers us as a gift is more than we can imagine. His promised salvation will bring about reconciliation amongst estranged family members, ease the pain of hurts, bind up hearts that are broken and rekindle lost love.

This is a season of waiting in joyful hope for the coming of our Saviour, Jesus Christ. At this time of year we are meant to be at peace with ourselves. Let us take a moment to think of family and friends who have gone ahead of us and rounded the corner on the road to eternal life. The pain of their loss has brought endless days of heartbreak and loneliness. However, they have gone no further from us than God, and God is very near.

Prayer of the Faithful

With confidence in the goodness of the God of love and the giver of salvation, we make our prayer.

1. We pray for the leaders of the church. May they lead by example and so help people to discover God in their lives.
   Lord, hear us.

2. We pray in this Advent season for all those people whose goodness we are inclined to take for granted. May we become more aware of their generosity towards us.
   Lord, hear us.

3. May all married people reach out gladly for your healing touch that brings love and peace into their lives.
   Lord, hear us.

4. We pray for those who are sick in mind and body and those oppressed by any need. Help them realise how near you are to all who cry out in their anguish.
   Lord, hear us.

5. For those who have died, especially N. and N., that they may find peace and discover rest in the kingdom of God.
   Lord, hear us.

God of grace, open our hearts and minds and make us a people who respond to your voice and obey your will. Help us to prepare a place for your Son in our hearts. We make our prayers in the name of Jesus the Lord. Amen.

3rd Sunday of Advent
First Reading: Zephaniah 3:14-18;
Second Reading: Philippians 4:4-7; Gospel: Luke 3:10-18

John the Baptist is one of the most intriguing and challenging characters in the entire bible. His curious figure is the centre of attention on our doorstep this morning. Unlike Jesus, who had a normal family upbringing, John left home while still a youth and went off to live a hermit's life of lonely austerity in the desert. There he was summoned by the Spirit to prepare a people, making them ready for the coming of the Lord. He preached in the wilderness and his trademark was a baptism of repentance for the forgiveness of sins. Out of curiosity, people from all over Palestine came to hear his blistering words about the wrath of God. His fiery message had an irresistible fascination and struck a chord that resounded through the whole countryside. He spoke powerfully to the sinful hearts of people who had turned from God and warned them that the time of judgement was near at hand. Many were convinced by his preaching, acknowledged their sinfulness and as a sign of their sincerity underwent a ritual cleansing in the waters of the Jordan. The Baptist was a humble man who knew his limits and he did not step beyond them. He spoke the truth to the people but he did not glorify himself. According to his own words, he was merely a messenger preparing the way for 'Someone who is more powerful than I am and whose sandals' straps I am not fit to undo.' The Baptist came to complete God's work of paving the way for the Lord's coming. He was the last and greatest of the prophets, a frontier man who linked the Old Testament to the New Testament.

John the Baptist is a fitting role model as we prepare in Advent for the coming of the Lord. The advice he gave to the people he baptised and who asked for guidance as to what they must do to prepare for the coming of the Lord, is applicable in our time. His words reach directly into our hearts. When soldiers, who ran roughshod over civilians, and tax collectors notorious for their exploitation, came forward for baptism he reminded them of their professional responsibilities as public servants and cautioned them to carry out their work with honesty, integrity and concern. Their dealings were to be carried out in a spirit of service without any display of raw power, trampling on the oppressed or exploitation of the vulnerable. Anyone with two tunics was to share with the man who had none. Possessions must be seen for what they are and the call to share them with the dispossessed and the deprived, is something we must tend to as an urgent priority, if the joy and peace of Christ is to be born into our lives this Christmas. Each of us knows what has caused us to drift away from God. It may be selfishness, not getting our own way, hurting others with unkind words or the pursuit of materialism.

John the Baptist stands before us, an Israelite who kept the promise of the Messiah alive in people's hearts. He calls us to give a practical expression to his message by waiting in joyful hope for the coming of our Lord and Saviour Jesus Christ. Who among us, with our never-ending problems wouldn't hunger for more joy in our lives? According to today's readings there is no reason for us to live our lives devoid of it. God is among us and the deep-rooted cause of our joy is awareness that he has come to save us. Joy is never far away but it often proves elusive and we miss it. The problem is that very often we go looking for it in far away places and in the spectacular, whereas all the time joy is to be found in the ordinary things, in everyday happenings and with ordinary people. It is to be experienced in the smile of a child, in the glow of the fire, in a letter from a friend and on the faces of people at a football match. We can also discover that we possess joy in the good we do and in our caring and sharing.

During this Advent season we return to the deep well of God's grace to encounter again the gift that we have received. We light the candles of Advent to shed some light in the darker recesses of our lives. With an unwavering trust, we pray that the light of Christ may show us our strengths and weaknesses and that the Child of Bethlehem will help us foster our better selves and be the disciples we aspire to become.

Prayer of the Faithful

Full of joy at the nearness of the Lord, we pray to the creator of all that is good and ask him to pour out the power of his strengthening love upon us.

1. We pray for those who have been given the spirit of leadership in the church. May they be wise and understanding and have the courage to follow the ways of God.
   Lord, hear us.

2. For all those who are blinded by materialism and experience no need for God in their lives. May they realise that the Lord is always passing by, especially in the guise of the poor who are in need of their help.
   Lord, hear us.

3. For those among us who still carry the hurts of childhood. May the Lord reach into our past to heal our wounds and enable us to discover a balanced view of life.
   Lord, hear us.

4. We pray for those whose lives have been broken by illness. May they regain their health and may our presence be a source of encouragement on their road to recovery.
   Lord, hear us.

5. For the bereaved of our community, especially those who have lost loved ones in the course of the past year. May they receive peace and comfort from those who share their grief.
   Lord, hear us.

God of splendour and glory, hear the prayer of your people. May the joy we feel in your presence overflow into our daily lives so that we may proclaim the greatness of your love through Christ, our Lord. Amen.

4th Sunday of Advent

First Reading: Micah 5:1-4;
Second Reading: Hebrews 10: 5-10; Gospel: Luke 1:39-45

One of the most joyful episodes in all of the gospels is the visit of
Mary to her elderly cousin Elizabeth. The story is so familiar that
we are inclined to overlook the deeper significance of the encounter. Both women were about to give birth in a miraculous
way. Mary had just received a message from the angel Gabriel
that she was chosen to conceive and give birth to the Saviour of
the world and that her aged cousin Elizabeth was preparing to
be the mother of John the Baptist. Along with her husband
Zechariah, who served as a priest in the temple at Jerusalem,
Elizabeth had prayed for a child all their married life. Finally in
old age, when all hope had faded away, Elizabeth is especially
blessed by God and their request is granted. Nothing could be
more natural after the annunciation, than Mary's desire to go
and visit her cousin, so that both of them could share the news of
their good fortune. The visitation was a rather remarkable in-
stance of caring and concern on the part of Mary. She undertook
this journey into the hills as an act of charity to her elderly
cousin, who was in need of reassurance about the promised
birth. Let us not forget that travelling in those days was neither
easy nor safe. Such a trip would have been a foolhardy under-
taking for a single girl in her late teens who was expecting. Mary
had a long and difficult road in front of her. The distance to
Elizabeth's house was a four-day caravan journey over the dirt
roads, mountain streams and stony treks of a hilly Judean countryside. Medieval artists have produced some wonderful paint-
ings of this particular event.

The meeting of the young Mary with the old Elizabeth was
indeed an extraordinary encounter. Good news becomes great
news when it is shared. No two women ever met, before or
since, with greater expectations. They are together caught up in
the drama of God's unfolding promise. We can picture the two
mothers-to-be running to greet each other, thrilled with excitement and overcome with joy at the good news that they ex-
change. As they shared each other's dreams, they had plenty of

cause to rejoice and wonder about God's marvellous works. Before Jesus came to the rest of the world at Christmas, Elizabeth had the extraordinary privilege of having the Christ child pay her a visit in the womb of Mary. It was so great an honour that the child she herself was carrying in her own body leapt for joy. That child would be named John and would grow up to be the last and greatest of the prophets – the messenger preparing the way for the coming of the Saviour. He was destined to be a frontiersman linking the old to the new and a beacon pointing people towards God's Son.

This period of time, in the run up to Christmas, is one of hectic activity. There is excitement in the air with Christmas cards, parties, visits and gifts all absorbing our attention and draining our energy. The spirit of the Christmas season is infectious and seems to catch hold of us before the actual day has arrived. It has a marked effect on many people who act differently and are more polite, generous and outgoing than at other times of the year. For a few days we forget our animosities, rid ourselves of bitterness and the whole world seems to be a better place. It is essentially a family feast and we do our best to put the necessary preparations in place so that we can be at home and part of the family circle for the occasion. What makes it a feast of the home is the realisation that God first made his home with us at this time of the year. He came among us and showed us that we are called to be children of God.

Advent is a time when we prepare ourselves spiritually for the coming of Jesus into our lives. It is a time of grace, when we accept that Jesus is the Saviour sent by God. In this gospel Mary shows us one obvious way of preparing for Christmas. Out of the goodness of her heart she visited an elderly cousin who was confined. Her visit brought great joy to both of them. There is no reason why we cannot follow her example with a visit to some sick or elderly person in the neighbourhood, who is lonely and in need of company.

Prayer of the Faithful

As we prepare to celebrate the birth of Christ our Saviour, we ask God the Father to make our hearts worthy dwelling places for his Son.

1. We pray for religious and civil leaders. May their manner of governing reflect gospel values and may they treat all people with respect and dignity.
   Lord, hear us.

2. We pray that our worshipping communities may be places this Christmas where those in need may find love, sympathy and support.
   Lord, hear us.

3. Let us pray that, like Mary, we may welcome the Son of God into our lives and so enter more deeply into the meaning of what we celebrate.
   Lord, hear us.

4. For the old, the sick and the lonely, that they may experience the presence of Christ this Christmas time.
   Lord, hear us.

5. For the dead, especially those we have known and loved and whose absence we feel at this family season.
   Lord, hear us.

Heavenly Father, look with favour upon your people, turn our hearts and homes into worthy dwelling places for your Son, whose birth we await with great joy. May we never cease to place our trust in you. We make our prayer through Christ, our Lord. Amen.

The Nativity of the Lord
First Reading: Isaiah 9:1-7;
Second Reading: Titus 2:11-14; Gospel: Luke 2:1-14

Christmas is a feast full of wonder and hope. What we celebrate is no less than God's entry into the world in human form. Despite our familiarity with the happening, this simple gospel story strikes a chord, touches something deep within us and evokes a response in every Christian heart. Our minds go back to the birth of a tiny baby, in a humble shepherd's sheltering place, somewhere in the hills near Bethlehem. Journeying in mid-winter, coping with large crowds, due to it being census time, and being in an unfamiliar place far from home when expecting a child, wasn't smooth or easy for Joseph and Mary. If anything, it was real hardship. Amidst the arrival of the newborn in a stable only fit for animals, there was pain as well as joy for all concerned.

Christ came quietly and without any fuss, born into a poor family in a humble cattle shed. There was no royal fanfare to announce his arrival. The shepherds keeping watch over their flocks by night were the only folk who noticed. The angel entrusted them with the glad tidings. 'Do not be afraid,' the angel said, 'I bring you good news of great joy, a joy to be shared by the whole people. Today a Saviour is born to you who is Christ the Lord.' The Messiah came among us in meekness and humility offering us his companionship, inviting us into the friendship of his own family circle. We are awe-struck that the maker of heaven and earth, he who called the universe into existence and sustains its every breath, should stoop down and touch our lives. 'The word became flesh and dwelt among us.'

As we keep vigil and await the birth of our Saviour we are united in spirit with Christians who have gathered through the centuries to celebrate this great feast. Looking in awe at the Christmas crib gives us a moment to come face to face with the child that lives in each one of us. Perhaps it's an opportunity to put ourselves back in touch with the source of wonder and imagination, by allowing the story of the Christ child to become our story as well. Christmas is the pinnacle of the year for children; they have been looking forward to this wonderful occasion with terrific excitement for weeks and will remember it for the rest of their lives. They associate it with the magical moments of sending letters to Father Christmas, receiving gifts and opening presents. At this time each year celebrations are called for and it is not only the decorations that are brought out of the cupboard but also family memories of our own childhood. This, more than any other celebration, is our family feast. We associate it with homecoming and there is nothing like a family gathered around the festive table to set the atmosphere. It is a time for being in the places we love with the people who mean so much to us. We spare a thought for those less fortunate than ourselves, those who for whatever reason have been unable to make it home this year, those hospitalised and those who are separated from family members due to unhappy domestic circumstances. Amidst all the joyful celebrations there will be many whose hearts are heavy and whose minds are elsewhere due to the absence of loved ones who have died and gone ahead of us on the road of life. It is only natural that we remember them at this time of year. Christmas prompts us to spare a thought for the poor and the hungry people of our society. The sheer abundance of our excessiveness is in marked contrast to those who are dependent on the crumbs that fall from our festive tables. Our feasting highlights their fasting. The real story of Christmas brings us discomfort because if we really want to discover God in Bethlehem we must visit the sick and the broken-hearted, the downtrodden and the outcasts of our society with whom he so closely identified. Bethlehem is not far from Jerusalem, and the crib is not far away from the cross.

Christmas speaks to the very depth of our being about the wonderful future on offer. It comforts us to know that we are sought after by God himself who in the guise of a child has come to save us. The infant birth pushes back the shadows of darkness assuring us that life has meaning because the light of the world is in our midst. Wherever we are at Christmastime, whether joy comes easily or not, we need to remember that Christmas is more than party going, gift giving and receiving. Jesus is coming to make his home in our hearts and to warm our lives by his presence.

Prayer of the Faithful

In the brightness of this Holy Night, as we prepare to celebrate the birth of Mary's child, we ask God the Father to listen to our prayer and to look kindly on our needs.

1. That the church's message of peace on earth and good will among all peoples may, like the angel's song, resound throughout every nation.
   Lord, hear us.

2. For our family and friends and all those we hold dear, that God may fill their hearts with joy and gladness this Christmas day.
   Lord, hear us.

3. For all who are absent from home and away from family and friends this Christmas. that they may receive a welcome wherever they are.
   Lord, hear us.

4. For all for whom Christmas is a burden, that they too may know joy and peace.
   Lord, hear us.

5. Through our personal charity may the poor, the sick and the lonely receive their rightful share of Christmas happiness.
   Lord, hear us.

6. We call to mind our deceased relatives and friends, especially those who were with us on Christmas last. May the Lord bring them into his kingdom of everlasting peace.
   Lord, hear us.

God of tenderness and compassion, as we celebrate the birthday of your Son may we be filled with his spirit and live as children of the light so that, when our earthly journey is over, we may come to the kingdom you have prepared for us through Christ, our Lord. Amen.

Feast of the Holy Family
First Reading: 1 Samuel 1:20-22, 24-28;
Second Reading: 1 John 3:1-2, 21-24; Gospel: Luke 2:41-52

For many of us the image of the Holy Family is a trouble free one where nothing ever went wrong, where peace and harmony prevailed and where there was perfection in every way. The truth is otherwise, because like every family before or since, Joseph and Mary had their own share of difficulties and problems and knew the stresses and strains of family life. They led as normal a life as anyone else, never thought of themselves as being different and treated Jesus as any parents would have treated a child in those times. Few young couples would have experienced the degree of hardship which confronted Mary and Joseph when they searched for shelter prior to Jesus' birth, let alone their frantic flight into Egypt to save their child from the wrath of king Herod and his army. They knew what it was like to be refugees in a strange country without money. On the way home from their Passover visit to Jerusalem Jesus goes missing. In this gospel we witness Mary and Joseph desperate with worry returning to scour the city and frantically search the streets only to finally track him down in the temple where he was instructing the elders. Any parent who has had the dreadful experience of losing their child in a crowded shopping centre or on a beach will know only too well how Mary and Joseph felt on this occasion. Jesus' reply to his mother's expression of anxiety, 'Did you not know that I must be busy with my father's affairs?' did not help matters.

Families are not perfect, but it is in that setting we experience the greatest delights and bitterest disappointments with people whom we know and trust. Nowhere else is our character more deeply fashioned, our basic belief systems more strongly developed and our fundamental feelings about religion, life and the world more deeply imprinted. The family is the first school of social living. We learn to understand the people of the wider world because we first learn to cope with the members of our family. In the family we are taught how to give and take, to argue and make up, how to work out frustrations, resolve tensions and what it means to loose graciously. In this environment we first discover that others are there for us and we must be there for them. It is the pain of life lived in relationships among the people with whom we can identify. The real dramas are the ones fought and resolved in the home, between parents and children, husbands and wives leading ordinary lives and trying to do their best in a difficult world. In this setting we grow and develop and find the encouragement and support to achieve our dreams. It is love that makes the family a real community of persons, each giving and taking according to ability and each regarded by the other as a gift from God to be accepted and cherished.

The first and most basic love in the family is the love between husband and wife. Parents teach mostly by example and their love can be seen in the faces of their children. There is a wealth of evidence from social commentators to show that children from healthy home environments are likely to have good self-esteem, do well in school and possess good social skills. How children experience love from their parents affects the way they tend to love others and enter into gratifying relationships. Children are among the most vulnerable members of society and how we treat them is one of the best measures of the kind of people we are. It is no secret that in our affluent world children have less of their parents' time and attention and less security at home than a generation or two ago. We have got to ask what type of adult world is it that indulges itself and neglects its children? To justify our behaviour we have invented the myths of 'quality time' to make up for the lack of real time spent with children and we have convinced ourselves that child-care is as good as parental care. Particularly tragic and a major new source of poverty is the loss of fatherhood which is only marginally remedied by the payment of child support. Generally speaking, the real misery for children in fragmented families is that they are fatherless. In our fastly changing society marriage is still the best option for raising children who can carry the scars of a broken home for a lifetime. It was God who gave the family its special meaning, dignity and worth by seeing to it that his own son was born into one. For good or bad the family is the seedbed of the future and the foundations for building a humane world.

Prayer of the Faithful

On the feast of the Holy Family we turn to God the Father and ask him to shower his blessings on all families everywhere.

1. We pray that the family of the church throughout the world may be an example and guide to the nations of the world in their search for harmony and peace.
   Lord, hear us.

2. For parents who have the all-important job of forming the up-and-coming generation. Help them to love their children and to guide them in the ways of faith.
   Lord, hear us.

3. For children who have been hurt or abused by adults. Help them find healing in their pain and forgiveness towards those who have harmed them.
   Lord, hear us.

4. For social workers and marriage counsellors: may they show compassion and understanding in dealing with the problems of married people.
   Lord, hear us.

5. Grant health where there is sickness; send help where there is poverty and healing where there is hurt.
   Lord, hear us.

6. For our departed brothers and sisters who believed in the power of God. May they come to know the joy of everlasting peace.
   Lord, hear us

Heavenly Father, convert our hearts into fit dwelling places for your Son. In our homes may we sympathise rather than criticise, praise rather than blame so that they may become places where your love and peace reigns. We make our prayer through Christ, our Lord. Amen.

2nd Sunday after Christmas

First Reading: Ecclesiasticus 24:1-2, 8-12;
Second Reading: Ephesians 1:3-6, 15-18; Gospel: John 1:1-18

The church is at pains to make us reflect a little more deeply on the real message of Christmas, which is the feast of the great beginning of our salvation, while she still has our seasonal attention and mood. The gospel, which is profoundly beautiful in its message, presents us with God's plan of salvation. The gift of God's life has been given to us in the person of Jesus, who came to earth to meet us in our humanity and made himself available to all. As we approach the crib, kneel down and embrace the mystery, the thought crosses our mind as to what the eternal God was thinking about when he decided to come among us. It was nothing less than a rescue operation to bring us out of the darkness of sin and bathe us in his own wonderful light. Jesus Christ became our brother for no other reason than sheer love and a desire to have us live in an intimate loving family relationship with him. Like a great star he comes down from heaven, lights up our darkened world and enables us to glimpse the mystery through the cloud of uncertainty. In Christ, we have a brother who loves us to the extent that he came among us as a man and shared not only our life, but our death as well. We are a privileged people for God has moved in with us and we now bear his image and likeness.

In this gospel passage John is at pains to point out that, beneath the sketchy surface details of the birth of Christ, there lies an overwhelming mystery. We ponder in amazement at the self-emptying of God, at the Almighty becoming the all-lowly, a child perched on his mother's knee, helplessly gazing out at us from a lowly manger. Jesus, first and foremost, is God joining himself to us in the flesh. He would walk in our shoes, share our kind of living, celebrate in our joys, weep in our tears, suffer in our sorrows and give thanks in our accomplishments. As a result, we are called to be his adopted children and heirs to God's heavenly kingdom. Christmas, at its deepest level, means we are part of the family of God. The turn of the year presents us with an opportunity to dwell on our Christian identity. If God has become man for our sakes, we must ourselves become more fully human and treat others as persons. To live life to the full we have got to be alert to all the possibilities of our humanity and understand the real purpose of our existence. Jesus frees us from the shackles of sin, which cling so easily, and indeed from death itself.

We are a new creation because God is truly one of us. Our mission is to accept Christ as revealed to us in our quarrelsome, battered, human family and become involved in his saving plan for the world. In his own time, many failed to welcome him; doors were slammed and there was no room for his message, because hearts were cold. There are those in every age who do not accept him and choose to live in darkness. Christmas tells us that it is in the ordinary happenings of life, as lived around us, that we find God. We express the true spirit of Christmas best when we offer help to those in need and bring hope to those who are lost. In this way we become a beam of light and a ray of hope piercing the darkness that surrounds so many lives. It would be a pity to prevent the light of God from shining in our lives by our failure to remove selfishness, hatred and bitterness from our hearts. Unless we keep that firmly in our minds and look for him, not just in the faces of family and friends, but also where there is poverty, want and despair Christmas will only be a sentimental pause at the end of a year and the challenge of Bethlehem will be lost completely.

Prayer of the Faithful

Called out of darkness into the wonderful light of God, we make our prayer to the Heavenly Father who has chosen us out of love, to be sharers in his eternal life, before the world began.

1. We pray that the church may joyfully preach the Good News and give hope and encouragement to all peoples.
   Lord, hear us.

2. For all the families in our community, that they may be blessed with good health and graced with happiness in the coming year.
   Lord, hear us.

3. For the children of the world, especially those who go hungry and are victims of violence and civil strife.
   Lord, hear us.

4. We remember the sick, the suffering, those who are anxious and the lonely. May the Lord show his warmth and graciousness to them. Lord, hear us.

5. For our dear departed loved ones who have died, that they may find light, happiness and peace in the kingdom of God.
   Lord, hear us.

Heavenly Father, make us worthy of your love and teach us to live as children of the light so that we may inherit the rich glories prepared for us from the foundation of the world. We ask this through Christ, our Lord. Amen

The Feast of the Epiphany

First Reading: Isaiah 60:1-6;
Second Reading: Ephesians 3:2-3, 5-6; Gospel: Matthew 2:1-12

With the Feast of the Epiphany we come to the end of the twelve days of Christmas. The festival closes on a high note with Matthew's colourful story of the Magi coming from the far corners of the earth to pay homage to the infant king. Who these men were and where they came from we are never likely to know, for their identity is never revealed. All we can do is speculate as to their origins. Just about the time Jesus was born, the sudden appearance of a bright star in the eastern sky gave rise to the expectation of the birth of a great leader. The popular belief among pagans of the period was that every important person had a special star, which rose when they were born and faded when they died. The appearance of this brightly shining star convinced these good and holy men to begin their spiritual adventure. What drew them to make the journey in the first place was their openness to the word of God as expressed in their searching for a more meaningful way to live their ordinary lives. Their pilgrimage of exploration into the unknown encountered many obstacles. It meant being uprooted and leaving behind the security and comfort of home. They were exposed to the fear of moving into unfamiliar territory, as the trek towards Bethlehem was faltering and uncertain. There must have been periods of doubt and times of confusion when they felt that their journey was leading nowhere. Often the light from the star was dim and distant and they were left to discern their pathway as best they could under darkened skies. Then there was the cunningness of Herod who felt threatened by the news of the infant birth and did his utmost to undermine their plans with his wickedness. Nevertheless they persisted in their search and sought diligently for the young child until they found him. The one thing the Magi were unprepared for was the poverty of the infant king born in a stable and lying on a bed of straw. Yet, because they saw with the eyes of faith, they were certain that this was the redeemer whom they were looking for. They humbly bowed down before the child and paid their respects with offerings of gold, frankincense and myrrh – gifts which expressed their belief in the true identity and life mission of the infant Jesus. Having reached their destination they returned home enriched by their discovery of the glory of God and the light of the world in such humble surroundings.

The message of the Epiphany is that God wants to show forth his extravagant love to all peoples without exception. His mercy, forgiveness and compassion are not restricted to an exclusive elite but are offered to everyone. All nations are called to share in Christ's glory. He is here for all and no one is excluded from his offer of peace. The Christian gospel is intended to reach across boundaries and speak to every human heart. Foreigners and outsiders are embraced with the same love as everyone else. While most of us travel to God by routes charted out by previous generations of faithful Christians, we should have the greatest respect for those who make the homeward journey in sincerity of heart by a different route. We meet God in each other especially in our frailty and brokenness.

This is not only a story of the past but a parable for every day as in some sense it is the personal story of each one of us. The searching of the Magi reaches across boundaries and finds echoes in all our hearts. Life is a journey we all have to make and a spiritual pilgrimage where we strive to find our true selves. Our journey to God may not require any physical travel but a journey inwards to our own depths. This journey to that quiet centre where one's life and spirit are united with the life and spirit of God is long and difficult. To reach that place is to be at home; to fail to get there is to be forever restless. We too are called to offer from the treasury of our lives whatever gifts we possess in the worship of the infant child. If Jesus is to be made known to all peoples, it will have to be through our efforts. This feast calls us to 'Rise up and look around!' and to recognise the Lord in our midst in ways we hadn't expected to find him.

Prayer of the faithful

Confident that he will grant our requests, we approach the Father, who made known to the Magi the birth of his Son by the light of a star, and ask for his guidance.

1. For the church throughout the world, that it may carry the light of Christ to people everywhere so that those who are searching may find the truth.
   Lord, hear us.

2. For the leaders of nations, that they may strive to promote justice and bring the peace of Christ into the world.
   Lord, hear us.

3. We pray for the ability to listen to, learn from and appreciate people who come from a different cultural tradition and who view life from another perspective.
   Lord, hear us.

4. We place before the Lord all the sick and aged members of our community. We ask him to look upon them with love and mercy. Lord, hear us.

5. That those whose earthly pilgrimage is over may have a place in God's kingdom of light and love.
   Lord, hear us.

God our Father, you sent your Son into the world to draw all people to the truth. Help us to proclaim the good news and may we never fail to listen to your voice. We make our prayer through Christ, our Lord. Amen.

The Baptism of the Lord
First Reading: Isaiah 40:1-5, 9-11;
Second Reading: Titus 2:2:11-14, 3:4-7; Gospel: Luke 3:15-16, 21-22

Christmas is over. After our touching school nativity play, along with our rousing carol service and meaningful midnight Mass, we sense a feeling of deflation, of coming down to earth and back to basics with no time to lose. It is as if the church does not want us to linger too long around the sentimentality of the manger. We are even asked to skip past those youthful years of growing up in Nazareth where Jesus was known locally as the son of Joseph the carpenter. Instead we are invited to focus our attention on the adult Christ who has a growing awareness of what his role and mission in life is to be and who has come to realise his special relationship with the Father. His meeting with John the Baptist at the banks of the river Jordan was no ordinary event. It was a moment of great significance and an important turning point in his life. It signalled an end to the long period of waiting in Nazareth and marked the beginning of his public ministry, which was accompanied by the sign of God's presence and approval. 'Heaven opened and the Holy Spirit descended on him in bodily shape, like a dove. And a voice came from the clouds, "You are my Son, the beloved; my favour rests on you".' The reign of God, restoring his wounded and broken creation, had begun. Christ was beginning his work as Saviour and taking on his shoulders our sadness, our sorrow and our sinfulness.

At his baptism he began a journey that would lead to the cross. It was a journey only God could accomplish for it meant washing away the sinfulness and healing the brokeness of humanity. Filled with the gift of the spirit, Jesus began his personal mission of preaching the good news, healing the sick, raising the dead and restoring sight to the blind. By emptying himself of power he, who was sinless, assumed our frail and limited nature in order to identify as far as possible with us in our plight. His passing through the murky waters of suffering and death on our account is an assurance that the things that are the death of us are no longer the end of us. His baptism was a statement that he was here with us and for us.

As we celebrate the great public beginning of Jesus we cannot but think of our own baptism which was the start of a journey in which we were commissioned as members of the Christian community to share in Christ's work of spreading the good news of the gospel. Baptism makes us sons and daughters of God by giving us an identity of belonging to his family, the church. Most of us have no recollection of the moment when, as infants, we were brought into church and carried to the font by our parents. On that occasion as the waters of baptism were poured over our head and we were anointed with the oil of chrism a commitment was spoken for us and our future was pledged to God. As adults we have to own those promises made on our behalf by becoming more aware of their implications. We must be serious about our obligation to live by a Christian set of values in a world that does not accept them. The way we live does make a difference. Each moment of life presents us with many different opportunities for living out our Christian faith. Jesus is not expecting great things of us. He wants us to quietly do the ordinary little things that come up on a daily basis. Once we do this, he somehow takes over and all kinds of wonderful things begin to happen. Unknown to ourselves we move out to others in ever wider circles. We make the discovery that little things seem to be much more important than they were before. At this moment in our lives we come to realise that there are people who need our help, who search for our guidance and who look for our love. Our baptismal calling teaches us not to be afraid to talk to them, to listen with understanding, to give them hope. Everyday, God comforts and heals the bodies and souls of his wounded people. The miracle is that through baptism God has chosen us to be his instrument of peace and hope by standing up for what is just and fair and reaching out to those who are imprisoned in any way.

Prayer of the Faithful

At his baptism in the River Jordan, strengthened by his Father's love, our Lord began his public ministry of preaching and teaching. Placing our trust in that same love, we make our prayer.

1. That the church may guide all Christians joined with your Son through baptism, to work together for the salvation of all peoples.
   Lord, hear us.

2. May the Lord inspire and bless our young people so that they may come to know the will of God for them and find strength and joy in following Christ.
   Lord, hear us.

3. For those who have been recently baptised: may their parents and godparents be true examples of faith in their lives.
   Lord, hear us.

4. Let us pray for doctors, nurses and all who work in our hospitals. May they bring encouragement and love in their ministry to the sick people under their care.
   Lord, hear us.

5. For those who have died, (especially N. and N.), may the Lord greet them as his beloved children.
   Lord, hear us.

God our Father, in the waters of baptism we died to sin and rose with Christ to become your adopted children. Strengthen us by the Spirit to do your work and to live in your presence. We make our prayer through Christ, our Lord. Amen.

1st Sunday of Lent
First Reading: Deuteronomy 26:4-10;
Second Reading: Romans 10:8-13; Gospel: Luke 4:1-13

Another Lent has dawned and fresh beginnings are at hand.
With it a new season of prayer, penance and fasting starts in the
church and everyday stretches into a few more moments of sun-
light. Every once in a while the chill in the air is replaced by a
soothing warmth which takes the edge off the biting wind. The
buds on the trees swell with the promise of something new because something old has died under the grip of winter. The
earth prepares to show us a new and gentler face. Each new
blossom is a growing hope and an assurance that we are precious in the eyes of God.

The fasting of Jesus in the desert and his struggle with the
powers of evil have caught the Christian imagination down
through the ages. So much so that it has inspired us to spend the
forty days of Lent trying to capture something of the spirit of
Jesus in the wilderness in order to assess our relationship with
God and renew our trust in him. The wilderness is not a romantic place nor is it a far away desert. It can be within ourselves
when a problem arises and we are in need of direction and at a
loss for proper moral guidance. The events in the wilderness
where Jesus was tempted to show allegiance to Satan were no
chance happenings. At the end of forty days, which saw Jesus
weak and vulnerable, the tempter makes his move. He begins to
test Jesus' relationship with the Father, inviting him to abandon
his mission to humanity. It would have been so easy for Jesus to
use his power for his own benefit and satisfy his hunger by turning stones into bread. We can't but admire his resolve in refus-
ing to let his body dictate to his spirit. He does not allow his feelings to influence his actions and refuses to make bread his priority. The temptation to pursue glory and to hunger after power
by becoming the political ruler of the entire world amounts to
shifting his allegiance to the devil. The final temptation is to become a Messiah of the spectacular by performing the dramatic
eye catching action of throwing himself from the pinnacle of the
temple and emerging unscathed. In that way he would seek at-

tention, earn adulation, impress the crowd and win their admiration. However, signs and wonders are no substitute for faith in his name.

The temptations of Jesus in the wilderness challenge us to face up to ourselves and to the deep down reality of sin in our lives and of our need for a change of heart. As long as we are alive we will be faced with temptation, for it is a universal human experience. Part of the tapestry of life is that good will always be tested by evil. It is comforting to know when temptation comes our way that Jesus was there before us. He was tempted, as we are tempted, like us in all things but sin. It is so easy to be led astray, to be dazzled by the riches of the world, and lose sight of the basic purpose of life. We are all impressed by the quick fix and the easy life, which are momentarily satisfying without taking into account what is of more permanent value. There is a wilderness and dark shadow within our being and despite our best efforts we fail to live up to what is expected of us. Self-importance, arrogance, pretence, and pride are but some of the demons that continue to drag us down.

Lent is a season for coming back to the Lord. We are often asked what are we giving up or going off for Lent? Maybe it is a time for getting back to the things we have neglected. We are encouraged to commit ourselves to the practice of prayer, fasting and almsgiving. Prayer can take many forms, like going to Mass frequently, reading the scriptures daily, reciting the rosary or being part of a prayer group. Fasting is one of the core disciplines of Christianity. Along with being part of the process for making amends for our sins, it is a traditional way of acknowledging one's dependence on God. If it does nothing else it reminds us that while one third of the world is suffering from over consumption the other two thirds are dying from hunger and malnutrition. The money we set aside for worthwhile charitable causes can bring freedom and a fresh start to the poorest of people. Lent is a time for drawing closer to God and through repentance, conversion and a change of heart to reflect on what he has done by bringing us salvation. In this way we prepare ourselves spiritually for the feast of Easter.

Prayer of the Faithful

As we begin our Lenten observance we are mindful of God's infinite mercy towards us and so we confidently call upon the Father for all our needs.

1. We pray for the leaders of the church, that through their example and encouragement they may inspire us to lead good and holy lives.
   Lord, hear us.

2. That during this holy season of Lent we may seek reconciliation with those from whom we are presently estranged.
   Lord, hear us.

3. That we may not hanker after the pleasures of material comforts or be blinded by the attraction of evil but hunger after spiritual values.
   Lord, hear us.

4. That those who are distressed by sickness, grief or worry may receive the consolation of your presence and the support of God's people in their time of need.
   Lord, hear us.

5. That the faithful departed may all enjoy a place in your kingdom.
   Lord, hear us.

Heavenly Father, pour out your blessing upon us. May this Lenten season of prayer, fasting and almsgiving be a time of spiritual growth in our lives. Help us to understand that when we fall, you love us still. We make our prayer through Christ, our Lord. Amen.

2nd Sunday of Lent
First Reading: Genesis 15:5-12, 17-18;
Second Reading: Philippians 3:17-4:1; Gospel: Luke 9:28-36

Jesus was a man who was close to nature. He knew the Lake of Gennesareth, the Jordan River, the Dead Sea and the hills of Judea. The fields the farmers tilled and the mountains the shepherds roamed held a special place in his heart. When he wanted to be on his own and away from the crowd he retreated to the mountains where he refreshed his spirit. Mountains offer a wider view not only of the countryside but also of life itself. They give us an overall picture of our petty world with all its preoccupations. The apostles Peter, James and John who were his closest friends accompanied Jesus on this particular occasion. While at prayer on the mountaintop a remarkable event took place. The physical appearance of Jesus changed dramatically and his countenance became brilliantly white in a way that bore no earthly resemblance. In his company were Moses and Elijah and they were discussing the fate awaiting him in Jerusalem. For the apostles who thought they knew Jesus very well this was an awesome encounter with the unfamiliar and a vision of Jesus in glory they had never imagined. They would never forget the look on his face as his divinity shone through in a way it had never done before. When a voice from the cloud proclaimed Jesus as God's beloved Son, the whole scene was almost too mysterious for human eyes to witness. The disciples' realisation that God was walking with them on this earth was beyond all their earthly expectations. The vision passed away and the road to Calvary lay ahead. The same three disciples who witnessed his moment of ecstasy would journey with Jesus to the Mount of Olives outside of Jerusalem. There, they would observe his agony in the garden of Gethsemane as he sweated blood, cried out in pain and pleaded with the Father to remove the cup of bitterness and get rid of the cross.

The moment of revelation is over and the apostles are back to reality, strengthened in faith by its memory for the dark future that lay ahead of them. This gospel points out that the glory of the Messiah can only be won at the cost of suffering and death.

Like Peter, most of us would prefer to remain on the hill of trans-figuration with Christ as our companion, away from the trials and tribulations of the real world. However, life is not like that, and the challenge is to be with Christ on our own hill of Calvary amidst the suffering of whatever valley of tears happens to come our way.

Lent is a time to be open to the ways in which God can bring us salvation. It is a grace given opportunity to immerse our-selves in the collective pain of our brothers and sisters in Christ. There is no escaping the suffering, poverty and trouble that sur-rounds us. We see it in infant faces deprived of the innocence of childhood and in young people who are made feel that they are worthless and of no value to society. Parents struggling to rear a family and make ends meet are in a similar state of desperation as are the old who are of no consequence and left on the scrap heap of life. This gospel points out that God is present in peo-ple's agony as much as he is in their ecstasy. In everyday life we have very real encounters with God. He is there in the unseen, behind the ordinary appearances of people and places. If we look closely enough we can discover that God's presence is wait-ing to be revealed in the hidden depths and ordinary events of our day, in the face of suffering and in the compassion of caring friends. We need only to open our eyes to witness these daily happenings.

It is important to remember that during his ecstasy on Mount Tabor and his agony in the garden of Gethsemane Jesus prayed. If we are to be open to the human face of Jesus in everyday events we must endeavour to become prayerful people. As prayer deepens and strengthens our friendship with God, we should give serious consideration to finding a few moments amidst the business of each day to be with the Lord. It may be as we are waiting in a queue or out for a walk or before we retire for the night. What's important is finding a sacred space, turn-ing up and allowing Jesus to reveal his presence to us. Only if we spend time and be alone with God in prayer will the light shine through and give us a glimpse of what the future holds for those who believe.

Prayer of the Faithful

On Mount Tabor, the Father said of Jesus: 'This is my beloved Son, listen to him.' As his beloved sons and daughters, we confidently place before him our needs.

1. We pray that the church leaders may continue to show the loving presence of Christ in the world by the example of their lives.
   Lord, hear us

2. Give us a ready ear and an open heart to accept the good news, so that we may radiate Christ's presence and reflect his joy.
   Lord, hear us.

3. That our young people may grow strong in faith so as to face the future with happiness and hope.
   Lord, hear us.

4. We pray for the sick and all those who care for them. May the spirit of God bring consolation, strength and healing into their midst.
   Lord, hear us.

5. We pray that the faithful departed may come to know God's glory in heaven.
   Lord, hear us.

Heavenly Father, fill our hearts with your love and keep us faithful to the gospel of Christ. Give us the grace to rise above our human weaknesses and grant what is for our good and your glory through Christ, our Lord. Amen.

3rd Sunday of Lent
First Reading: Exodus 3:1-8, 13-15;
Second Reading: 1Cor 10:1-6, 10-12; Gospel Luke 13:1-9

When tragedy invades our lives and disaster strikes it can shake us to the core, fill us with fear, leave us searching for explanations and inevitably wanting to know why. The Israelites in the time of Jesus more often than not saw the vengeance of God at work in such unforeseen calamities. The widespread belief in times of flood, famine, plague and pestilence was that this was God's way of venting his anger and of punishing the victims who were simply reaping the rewards of their sinfulness. When queried about the reason for King Herod's ruthless killing of the Galileans offering sacrifice in the temple, Jesus rejects this notion of divine retribution for sinfulness and states that personal misfortune and random disaster can befall anyone. These events are not willed upon us. On the contrary, we can be confident that God who is compassionate and consoling does not abandon his people in their distress. He does not leave them to fend for themselves but suffers when his people endure misery, hardship and death.

The point that Jesus does emphasise is the sudden unexpected nature of such happenings and the importance of being reconciled with God and of being ready to meet our maker in case such a disaster might occur. This is very good advice because time is not our own. Life on earth is fragile, we can not know what the future holds and there is a sense in which death is always close at hand. In good times and bad we should turn to God for protection and forgiveness for we know neither the day nor the hour when we stand alone in his presence.

The story of the fig tree gives us a heartening glimpse into the mind of God who patiently watches as we mess up our lives. He continues to have confidence in us long after we have lost hope in ourselves. With the best will in the world, we cannot get through a day without making mistakes in our work, without falling foul of people and failing to recognise goodness and give credit where credit is due. Lent is a grace filled time to take stock of our lives, recognise our sinfulness and avail of the window of opportunity this holy season provides for repentance. One of the greatest enemies of the moral life is putting things on the long finger and waiting until tomorrow to do something. Such a person is forever looking forward to the right moment and the golden opportunity that never arrives. Someone said that life is what happens when something else is planned. The great mistake is to think that we are in control. All things considered, few of the really important occurrences of any person's life are programmed. The truth is that the most significant things happen among the commonplace and when least expected. It is a risky business putting repentance off to a later date because we have no idea how long our moment of grace will last.

It is the appearance of the golden moment among the ordinary that makes it extraordinary. That is why it is important to avail of the present time to grow closer to God and our neighbour by doing whatever good we can. Wouldn't it be a pity to let the present pass by and go unnoticed? The poet, John Greenleaf Whittier, expressed it this way: 'Among the saddest words of tongue and pen, the most regretted is, it might have been.' At the close of every day which is a God given gift and an opportunity to grow in grace, it is worth reflecting on what good we could have done and neglected to do.

In the Palestine of the gospels there was an abundance of fig trees which were renowned for the fruit they produced. In today's parable when the owner came looking for fruit, he was naturally disappointed and concluded the tree was only depleting the soil and would never bear fruit. Nevertheless he was prevailed upon to give it one more chance and leave it in the soil for another year. We have been given a patch of ground to cultivate and ample opportunity to bear fruit. Like the fig tree we are prone to failure and do not always produce what is demanded. The expectation is to redeem ourselves by producing the fruit of good living in our family life, in our community involvement and in our place of employment. On judgement day when we come face to face with God, we will be invited to give an account of our stewardship and asked what purpose was served by our presence in the world.

Prayer of the Faithful

Confident of his constant and supporting presence within us, we now make our prayer to the Lord who is slow to anger and rich in mercy and compassion.

1. We pray that all who exercise authority in the church may proclaim the truth with courage and be kind and merciful towards all whom they serve.
   Lord, hear us.

2. For all whose lives are empty of good deeds, may they produce the fruits of patience, generosity and peace.
   Lord, hear us.

3. We pray for ourselves that our hearts might be renewed by a deep conversion this Lent.
   Lord, hear us.

4. We ask the Lord to bless our sick friends and relatives. May they receive the healing power of Jesus Christ through the care and concern of those around them.
   Lord, hear us.

5. We pray for those who have died recently: may God take them to himself and may they live in his presence forever.
   Lord, hear us.

Lord our God, heal our ills, forgive our sins and help us to realise your goodness towards us. Crown us with your love and compassion so that we may live our lives for you. Amen.

4th Sunday of Lent
First Reading: Joshua 5:9-12;
Second Reading: 2 Cor 5:17-21; Gospel: Luke 15:1-3, 11-32

The art of storytelling is as ancient as the hills and is part of the oral tradition of every culture. Even in our age of instant communication the story is still a tremendous means for conveying an important message. Jesus was a gifted storyteller who used parables to great effect. The account of the prodigal son, one of the most beautiful and meaningful parables, is a brilliantly crafted masterpiece with a strong element of human interest. Worried parents anxiously waiting for their errant children to come home is a familiar occurrence in every generation and strikes a chord in all our hearts. We have no difficulty in picturing this young man with itchy feet who is restless, in pursuit of pleasure, ready for action and down right bored out of his mind, with the dull routine of family life. Maybe we have experienced this situation ourselves! Fired by a longing for excitement and adventure he packs his bags, turns his back on home and off he goes to live it up and pursue a reckless life of debauchery. The outcome is predictable – high living, low women, fair weather friends and foul booze. When his money runs out it isn't long before all kinds of troubles begin to plague him. The good times come to an end and he finishes up a penniless stranger in a foreign land. He becomes empty, disillusioned and disenchanted. Worse still, having sunk to desperate depths of depravity, he becomes a slave reduced to feeding swine and filling his stomach with the swill the animals were feeding on.

There is nothing like hunger to sharpen the mind and bring a person to their senses. Down on his luck he has time to reflect on what he, as a son from a fine home, is doing in rags and filth. It is a rapid and painful awakening. A lot of things need straightening out and the very thought of what he has thrown away stops him in his tracks. Remembering what it used to be like at home sets in motion a line of thought that brings him to his senses and searching for a way to return. Ashamed and disgraced there is nothing for it but to face the music and set off for home unaware of what reception might be in store for him. He can't believe his luck when his father, disregarding convention, runs forward with outstretched arms to greet him. Little does he realise that his father has spent all the years he was away waiting, watching, praying and hoping for his return. When he starts to make an apology the father will have none of it. He had every reason to be angry and refuse to accept his son back but the intensity of joy experienced at his return was such that his words were of love not of reproach. He instructed the servants, 'Bring out the best robe and put it on him; put a ring on his finger and sandals on his feet. Bring the calf that we have been fattening and kill it; we are going to have a feast.'

Not everyone is happy with the homecoming. The elder son on learning that his runaway, good for nothing brother has returned to a hero's welcome is miffed, angry, bitter with envy and refuses to join in the celebration. When the father tries to persuade him to come into the banquet hall and enter into the mood of the party he pours out the resentment of a lifetime. His lament is that of a loyal and dutiful son who has done nothing to disgrace the family name. He has never received any recognition for his goodness and feels cheated.

This story is told in so many different ways in our own lives, in our growing up and coming to terms with the joys and struggles of life as we find it. We can detect traces of both brothers in our makeup. There are shades of the younger one in the wildness of rebellious youth, which wants to grab all and try everything that is forbidden. Like the unforgiving older brother who was harsh and revelled in resentment we harbour hatreds, cling to grudges and nurse grievances. In our mean-spiritedness it is easy to become judgemental, lack compassion and forget that a heart without mercy is a heart without love.

The Father in the story is the picture of God, all the time watching, waiting and reaching out in love to his erring children with extraordinary warm-hearted forgiveness. There are no words to describe God's goodness and how his presence gives courage and dignity to broken lives. Whether our hurts are great or small, his healing grace is stronger than sin and always there for the asking. No story tells us more about the extent of God's compassion, the scope of his merciful love, and the extraordinary lengths he has gone to, to restore our broken relationship with him. God holds no grudges. His power is in kindness and no sinner is ever written off or considered beyond redemption. While harsh judgement belongs to this world, infinite compassion belongs to God who never gives up on his family. The parable challenges us to act like the father and let people see in our own lives something of what God is like.

Prayer of the Faithful

Ever mindful of the Father's forgiveness and compassion we gather as his wayward children and place our needs and concerns before him.

1. We pray that the leaders of the church may effectively announce God's mercy and forgiveness throughout the world.
   Lord, hear us.

2. For ourselves that, like the compassionate Father, we might have a more forgiving attitude to those who go astray.
   Lord, hear us.

3. That we may have the grace and courage to repent and seek reconciliation whenever our actions are the cause of conflict and suffering to other people.
   Lord, hear us.

4. We pray for those who are sick in body, mind or spirit: may they be comforted by the Lord's healing touch.
   Lord, hear us.

5. For those who have died: that they may enjoy eternal rest and perpetual light in heaven.
   Lord, hear us.

God of mercy and compassion, hear the prayers of your sinful people. Enlighten our minds and hearts so that all we think, say and do may be in conformity with your saving will. We make our prayer through Christ, our Lord. Amen.

5th Sunday of Lent
First Reading: Isaiah 43:16-21;
Second Reading: Philippians 3: 8-14; Gospel: John 8: 1-11

We can picture this early morning scene of Jesus sitting on a bench in the temple porch instructing listeners and answering their questions when he is rudely interrupted by the commotion caused by an irate group of Scribes and Pharisees who force their way into the gathering. They have dragged with them a woman caught in the very act of committing adultery and unceremoniously fling her at his feet. It is an ugly spectacle of dreadful cruelty as she stands in full view of everyone with clothes torn, dishevelled hair, frightened, disgraced and ashamed. The cards are stacked against her. Their treatment of this powerless woman is appalling. With breathtaking arrogance they callously use her for their own ends without the slightest regards for her feelings. Nothing can justify the conduct of these so-called pillars of society who are seen at their worst as they stand around the woman in an accusing circle. Worse still, she is nothing in their eyes, only a pawn in the game they have chosen to discredit Jesus and put him in a no win situation. If he called for death by stoning, Jesus would have broken Roman Law. If he let the woman go, he would have broken the Mosaic Law. They have caught Jesus in a neat dilemma and gloatingly wait for his answer. Dismayed by the insincerity of his accusers Jesus refuses to be trapped in the net that has been sprung to trick him. He stoops down and lets his fingers wander idly in the dust of the temple floor. The tables are turned when he straightens up and clearly announces, 'If there is one of you who has not sinned, let him be the first to throw a stone at her.' Challenging them to examine their conscience and check their own behaviour proves to be the parting of the ways as one by one they slink away burdened by the truth that they are sinners too. With respect and compassion Jesus turns to the woman, who was more sinned against than sinning, and in a moment of delicate beauty and gentle tenderness restores her dignity. His glance of love heals and he affords her the opportunity to begin again with the words, 'Neither do I condemn you, go away and sin no more'. The woman is being told to forget the past and look forward in hope to a new life.

We are familiar with the saying that people in glass houses should not throw stones and the main thrust of the story as far as we are concerned is to refrain from being judgemental, pointing the finger and spreading scandal. Knowing our own shortcomings we would do well to avoid condemning others. The fundamental difference between the woman caught in adultery and ourselves is that we have broken rules and have had the good fortune not to be found out. Are we not being self-righteous when we take pride in dragging a neighbour's reputation in the mud under the pretext of being honest and speaking the truth? Have we forgotten that the failings we spot in others are normally carried in some form within ourselves? Why do we expect perfection in other people when our own faults are so glaringly obvious? Living the Christian message is all about how we behave towards our fellow human beings. The self-righteous streak of the Scribes and Pharisees is alive and well in every worshipping congregation.

This is a gospel story about salvation, of sin committed and sin forgiven. Nowhere is the saving power of God more evident than in the forgiveness of sin. He reaches out to hearts in ways beyond explaining. God does not look at our faults or failings but expresses his belief in our inner goodness. We need to acknowledge our sins if we are to be forgiven. Jesus offers all who come to him the opportunity to turn away from wrong doing, to put the past behind, to be forgiven and embark upon a new life. All we have got to do is to open our hearts to receive his grace.

As our Lenten season draws to an end we should give added thought to our sins by taking a close look at our lives in order to determine the direction we are taking. Where have we come from and where are we going? Ours is a journey into the God who is perfect love, perfect understanding and perfect forgiveness. Like the woman in the gospel we may have to make certain adjustments if we are to get to know the Lord who looks beyond our present situation and sees a person in need of his forgiveness, love and grace.

Prayer of the Faithful

With joy in our hearts we make our prayer to the Father who is full of tender mercy and loving kindness towards sinners.

1. We pray that our Holy Father and the leaders of the church may continue to be a clear sign of God's loving mercy to all humankind.
   Lord, hear us.

2. Help us to be kind, understanding and forgiving and to re-frain from being critical and passing judgement on other people's faults.
   Lord, hear us.

3. For those who are enclosed in a bitter and hurtful past: may they experience the healing peace of Christ's forgiveness.
   Lord, hear us.

4. May we show kindness, understanding and compassion to-wards the sick and suffering in our neighbourhood.
   Lord, hear us.

5. We pray for those who have died, that the Lord may wel-come them into the joy of his kingdom.
   Lord, hear us.

Heavenly Father, we thank you for giving us your Son to be our Redeemer. Heal and strengthen our wounded hearts. Come to us in our need and send your Spirit upon us so that we may centre our lives on Jesus who lives and reigns forever and ever. Amen.

Passion Sunday

First Reading: Acts 10:34, 37-43;
Second Reading: Colossians 3:1-4; Gospel: John 20: 1-9

Gathered in our churches this weekend our attention is focused on Jerusalem and the hill of Calvary, as we prepare to re-enact the final scenes of Jesus' passion, death and resurrection. Holy Week contains the most beautiful liturgy of the church's year and the unfolding story of anguish, betrayal and pain provides us with an opportunity to involve ourselves in the drama and not just to remain as passive onlookers. The narrative begins with the dramatic scene of Jesus coming over the crest of the hill at the Mount of Olives riding on a colt. As the procession moves off the enthusiastic crowd throw their cloaks on the ground and wave branches of palm in the same way their ancestors would have done for a king. The disciples enter the spirit of the occasion by praising God, singing hymns and at the top of their voices proclaiming Jesus as the Messiah. However, not everyone loved the parade with its triumphal overtones. The religious leaders regarded Christ's manner of entry into the city as a deliberate and public act of defiance and were intent on stamping out his influence. He was a troublesome nobody who stirred the common people with talk of a kingdom of justice.

It did not take long for the mood to change and the welcome to turn into rejection. We take comfort in the depth of Jesus' love as he shares the Last Supper with the apostles. Immediately afterwards, we are quickly transported to scenes of agony, betrayal and arrest in the Garden of Gethsemane where the perspiration pouring down the Saviour's face became large drops of blood falling to the ground. Betrayed by a kiss, handed over as a result of Pilate's cowardice, crowned with thorns and shouldering a cross, Jesus begins his painful journey to the hill of Calvary. Along the route, where he suffered merciless cruelty and was brutally beaten, he remains a consoler and healer for the women who wailed and mourned openly at his plight. Not once did he, the innocent one, retaliate, return evil for evil, or strike back. On the contrary, he offered forgiveness to his executioners and promised paradise to the good thief. He had come to fulfil a mission and he could not be at peace until that mission was completed. We have a saviour who was crushed for our sins, convicted as a criminal and nailed to a cross where, on the brink of despair, he endured a sense of abandonment and desertion by the Father, that made him cry out 'My God, My God, why have you forsaken me?' Nevertheless, it is through the cross that Jesus lovingly does the will of the Father. All of this happened because 'He came that we should have life and have it to the full.' His death has put us at rights with God and given us a fresh start. The cross has an eloquence that reduces us to silence and leaves us to ponder on the limitless lengths God is prepared to go for our sake.

There is suffering in all our lives and we can all relate to physical pain. If we are to follow Christ, we must carry this cross, however falteringly or feebly. No one can escape his or her personal Calvary. Throughout history the suffering of Jesus has been a source of comfort, strength and inspiration to countless people in their time of pain. We can scarcely call ourselves Christians and not be moved by the poignant story of Mary during these last days, when she followed her son all the way to his death on the cross. She was his mother and must have agonised, as she looked on powerless to save him. Think of her sorrow on receiving the lifeless body of her Son, after it was taken down from the cross. It is a haunting image that touches something deep within us.

This is an opportunity to look beyond outward appearances and enter Holy Week in the company of the poor, the broken hearted and those who live on the edges of society where the needy are neglected and despair seems to hold sway. Like Simon of Cyrene we can offer a helping hand to assist the weary, nourish the weak and support those who are powerless, who count for nothing and are crushed by human indifference. In a strange way the word of God is alive as we react to it. Through putting its message into practice in our daily lives we follow Christ more closely and are assured that if we share in his suffering, we shall most certainly be glorified with him.

Prayer of the Faithful

Following the example of Jesus who, in the glory of his passion offered up prayers to his Father, aloud and in silent tears, we approach the Father with our petitions and the needs of the church.

1. That the leaders of the church may by the example of their lives give hope and encouragement to those who suffer on account of their faith.
   Lord, hear us.

2. Give us a new appreciation of the passion and death of Jesus so that we may follow in his footsteps, seeking not to be served but to serve and to offer our lives in simplicity and kindness.
   Lord, hear us.

3. For those who work to alleviate suffering in the world so that all of God's children may be able to live in freedom and dignity.
   Lord, hear us.

4. That the sick may draw strength from the example of Jesus and bear their sufferings with courage and love.
   Lord, hear us.

5. For those who have died: that they may rise in Christ who, on the cross, conquered death.
   Lord, hear us.

Heavenly Father, help us to welcome Jesus into our hearts and into our lives. Teach us to be humble, as he was humble and to be ready to carry our cross and journey to Jerusalem with him. We make our prayer through the same Christ, our Lord. Amen.

Easter Sunday
First Reading: Acts 10:34, 37-43;
Second Reading: Colossians 3:1-4; Gospel: John 20:1-9

Can you imagine how grief stricken Mary of Magdala must have been that first Easter morning as she hurried to the tomb of Jesus? Clutching in her hands a jar of precious ointment, her thoughts were solely on anointing his lifeless body in preparation for final burial. As soon as she noticed that the stone had been rolled back she feared the worst and in a state of shock ran to tell Simon Peter. Breathless and incoherent, she blurted out, 'They have taken the Lord out of the tomb and I don't know where they have put him.' The empty tomb seemed to add to her sorrow, depriving her of the last shred of comfort that caring for his body might offer. Peter and John were likewise confused, as they set out to find what happened, but on entering the tomb something within them changed as they gazed at the scene. At a glance they could see the body was missing. There was no sign of an intruder and with the burial robes and linen wrappings neatly folded, it gradually dawned on them that the absence of Jesus' body was not of human doing. Into the tomb had been placed a pierced and broken body; out of it emerged a living person. Slowly but surely the truth began to sink in and the disciples took their first step in recognising the resurrection. The gospels tell us how in the days that followed, Jesus appeared in their midst, speaking to the disciples, walking in their presence, sharing a meal and breaking bread in their company. Gradually they come to realise that everything that Jesus has said and done is indeed true.

Easter is a time when all of nature is blooming, when newness of life seems to be standing on tiptoes eager to reveal itself. The death of winter has passed and everything in the world around us is reawakening. It would be really sad if our inner spirit did not share in this great happening. Like the first believers we come to the tomb expecting to find death but are surprised to discover a place where new life has begun. The good news is that the Risen Christ has launched a new power into the world, giving us hope and grounds for satisfying our deepest longings. The truth of Easter is so vast that our minds need to be stretched in order to receive it. This is a day to embrace the living presence of Christ among us who gives a reason for living and a hope in dying. Easter holds out an invitation for all of us gathered in the church this morning to open our hearts to the Risen Christ and allow change to take place in our lives. It may mean that we have got to face up to some of the things that we don't particularly like about ourselves and how we see our behaviour as individuals. It could be that up to the present moment we have channelled too much of our energy into being angry, holding grudges or being resentful of the hand we have been dealt in life. Easter is telling us to roll back the stone and let go, that there is little to be gained by lamenting the past but to look to the future with renewed hope and begin again. Our task is to bring the Easter spirit to life in a suffering world. If we care to look around us, we will find in our midst the disheartened, the discouraged and the terminally ill crying out for attention. Dispensing love is one of the most wonderful things we can do. Giving of our time for a good cause brings with it the rich pleasure of doing something meaningful. Trying to help others in some shape or form makes our lives immensely happy. In a world that has grown selfish, thinking of other people can be a life-changing experience. The work to be done is considerable. The effort needed is great. However, the sense of achievement and sheer enjoyment found in the process cannot be denied.

On a more personal level, for those who have to live with the pain of loss, which is their own Good Friday, Easter encourages us to keep on hoping. It tells us that even although life is marked with uncertainties, in the midst of our troubles we are never to give up that we will get through. There is light at the end of the tunnel because the God of Easter says, 'Trust me. I am with you always.' Easter wakens us anew to the truth that there is a space within each of us which only God can fill.

Prayer of the Faithful

On this Easter Day, with renewed confidence in the love of God the Father for his children, we present our needs and those of the church.

1. We pray for the leaders of the church, that the Risen Lord will fill their daily lives with joy, love and peace.
   Lord, hear us.

2. That all the baptised may recognise their common dignity as children of God and respond generously to his love, which has been poured into their hearts by the Holy Spirit.
   Lord, hear us.

3. For ourselves, that the joy and peace of the risen Lord may fill our hearts and change our darkness into light and our doubts into faith.
   Lord, hear us.

4. For the sick and the suffering, that they may be gladdened and comforted by the good news of Jesus' resurrection.
   Lord, hear us.

5. For those who have died, that they may enjoy the fullness of life won for them by Christ.
   Lord, hear us.

Heavenly Father, we thank you for giving us this Easter Day, which has renewed all humankind. Keep us faithful to the new life you have given to us. We ask this through Christ, our Lord. Amen.

2nd Sunday of Easter

First Reading: Acts 5:12-16;
Second Reading: Rev 1:9-13, 17-19; Gospel: John 20:19-31

There is a Polish proverb which says that to believe with certainty we must begin by doubting. On the evening of the first day, when Jesus appeared to the apostles in the privacy of the upper room and showed them his hands and his side, Thomas was not present. He was so broken hearted that he had chosen to be alone in his grief, searching for an answer to the let down he suffered on Good Friday, when Christ was led away to be crucified. His dreams were shattered and he was a deeply troubled man who wondered how to go about rebuilding his broken world. Thomas was certain that Jesus was dead and to listen to the rumours that were doing the rounds about the empty tomb and the appearance of Christ behind locked doors did not help matters. No one could have wanted to see Jesus alive more than Thomas but in his struggle to find meaning in his hour of loss he was unwilling to believe the testimony of the other apostles. Words would never be enough to test the truth of what he wanted to believe. Only a personal encounter with the Risen Christ could convince him of such a happening. 'Unless I see the holes that the nails made in his hands and can put my finger into the holes they made, and unless I can put my hand into his side, I refuse to believe.' Thomas had demanded a sign and soon afterwards he got all the proof he needed. The Lord is more than willing to oblige and meets him at the point of his difficulty. As Thomas sees and touches the Lord's wounds, a light shines through his despair bringing about a startling and dramatic change. He recognises a truth he was unable to see beforehand and his journey from unbelief to belief is complete.

The phrase, 'a doubting Thomas' is part of our everyday language but although we may judge him harshly, by getting the proof he sought, Thomas has done us all a favour. He was right to ask the questions he did, for his words echo our own hesitant belief and lingering doubts and as a result has made us better believers. His doubts are of more value to the church than the spontaneous belief of the other apostles. The faith being asked of him was more demanding than the faith of those who had actually encountered the Risen Lord. Thomas stands for all those who have not seen the Lord but are called to believe in him, on the witness of others. This gospel is a story for everyone as it builds a bridge between those disciples who were present on Easter evening and saw Jesus and those like ourselves who have not seen him. The first disciples had the singular privilege of knowing Jesus, of seeing what he did, hearing what he preached and being healed by him. While we have no experience of the physical presence of Jesus, nevertheless our understanding of him is kept alive, linked through time and a great chain of faith that goes back to the apostles who were commissioned to share their faith with others. Favour with God does not come through seeing, but in trusting the words of the apostles.

From the very first Easter morning, the resurrection of Jesus was met with doubt and disbelief. However, it was the appearance of the resurrected Christ that set alight the flame of Christian faith and fired the apostles to proclaim the Risen Jesus. Living in an age where all the old supports and certainties are being questioned faith is not easy for any of us. Furthermore, we are so caught up in the material comfort of modern lifestyles, in a world of fashion and fads that we have precious little time to reflect on the meaning and purpose of life except in moments of personal crisis. The good thing about doubt is that it makes us look deeply within ourselves and reflect on what we believe. Nobody can do our believing for us. We each have to make our own journey and come to our own personal faith in Jesus. It is inevitable that our faith will be tested when we are confronted by difficulties and it is in such times that we need encouragement and support. Sometimes people come to faith on the evidence of the Lord's life as they see it alive in our believing community. There are those among us whose presence is a healing touch, whose smile warms our hearts and who bring with them wherever they go, the peace of Christ which came on that first Easter evening and filled the hearts of the disciples with joy. In these people we can see at work the wonder of the Risen Lord which echoes the words of Thomas, 'My Lord and my God.'

Prayer of the Faithful

Having listened to the words of scripture we now raise our hearts and minds to God so that he may touch our lives, heal our hearts and restore our faith.

1. That the leaders of the church may be a powerful sign of the Lord's peace and reconciliation at work in the world.
   Lord, hear us.

2. For those who have never heard of Christ, that his light may shine in their hearts, guide their steps and bring meaning and purpose to their lives.
   Lord, hear us.

3. For those who are weak in faith, that they may continue to grow in the love of the Lord in spite of their doubts and difficulties.
   Lord, hear us.

4. That the sick and those who suffer from disability may experience the comfort and healing power of the Easter message.
   Lord, hear us.

5. That all those who have died may share in the new life of the Risen Lord.
   Lord, hear us.

Heavenly Father, help us always to be faithful to the new life that you have given us. May the peace of Christ take hold of our hearts and minds and may we always enjoy your friendship. We make our prayer through Christ, our Lord. Amen.

3rd Sunday of Easter
First Reading: Acts 5:27-32, 40-41;
Second Reading: Rev 5:11-14; Gospel: John 21:1-19

The backdrop to one of the loveliest scenes in the life of the Risen Christ takes place by the lakeside of Galilee, not far from the spot where a few years earlier Jesus had invited his disciples to leave their nets and come follow him. The Risen Lord is standing at the water's edge, tending a charcoal fire, while dawn is breaking on the eastern sky. Approaching the shore in a boat are seven of his most trusted disciples. They are back at their nets, at what was their former livelihood and have spent the night fishing. The empty net drifting alongside the boat is proof that they are out of luck and their mood is far from cheerful. They have dragged the lake all night and, without anything to show for such hard work, they are wet, weary, cold and hungry. The stillness of dawn is broken by a voice from the shore telling them to cast their net one last time, as there was a shoal of fish on the starboard side of the boat. The apostles are stunned at the size of their catch. When they are invited to come and have breakfast, Peter suddenly realises that the mysterious helper is Jesus and he leaps overboard into the water in his eagerness to be the first to greet the Master. The other disciples were so overcome that they hardly spoke.

This lakeside breakfast echoes the miracle of the loaves and fishes when Jesus declared himself to be the bread of life. As is often the case with memorable meals, it was not just the food that was important but the company and the friendship that was shared. On the dawn of that new day Peter is brought out of his darkness, healed of his guilt and afforded an opportunity to affirm his love for the Lord. Before the crucifixion Peter had not exactly distinguished himself. The memory of his cowardice during the trial of Jesus, when he was caught out lying by a servant girl, must have been uppermost in his mind. Restored, renewed and rock-like the disciple, who failed the most, pledges his loyalty and turns this moment into a beautiful expression of loving service. Having been given the role of shepherd of the flock and commissioned to be the cornerstone of Christ's church, Peter is told that like his master he will pay for his commitment with his life.

Everyone in this church has had from time to time the experience of crushing disappointments, which weigh us down. We may face disappointment in a relationship, failure among our children, an upset with close friends or frustration at our work. The hurt is painful and the ache will not go away. Our defences are down and we haven't the will to put up a fight. With failure staring us in the face we lose our confidence, retreat within ourselves and seek comfort in false securities. Like the apostles in this gospel story we have sunk into the darkness of night where nothing is happening. We are living in a depression as if the resurrection never took place and are sorely in want of encouragement. We need to listen out for the sound of a voice coming from the shores of eternity beckoning us to try something new, to take a different direction and search for a new dawn. The good news of Easter is that Jesus is alive, watching over us and more interested in our future prospects than in our past failures. The daily challenge is to move forward, recognise the Lord in the ordinary events of our lives and stop trying to find contentment, peace and happiness in the wrong places. Like Peter we are no longer caught in the mesh of our own murky past, our faults and our failures. We have been freed, not just for the hereafter but for the here and now. We are much more able to operate effectively in our daily lives because we are not weighed down by the sins we have committed and the good deeds we have neglected to do. We can reach out to others because the Risen Lord reached out to us. We can be generous to the poor and the oppressed, to our neighbours and to the old, simply because Christ has been so kind to us who have deserved nothing. Ours is a life made new by the Risen Lord. We are children of the resurrection.

Prayer of the Faithful

Mindful that we are sent on the same mission as Peter, we turn to the Father and ask him to strengthen our faith.

1. We pray that our Holy Father and all who have been given special leadership roles within the church may exercise their responsibility as representatives of the Good Shepherd with courage and compassion.
   Lord, hear us.

2. That our young people might grow strong in faith so that they may face the future with joy and hope.
   Lord, hear us.

3. We pray for ourselves that we may proclaim the gospel by striving to follow the Risen Lord and reflect his glory in all we say and do.
   Lord, hear us.

4. For the sick that they may embrace the suffering that comes their way and find in the cross of Christ an opportunity for spiritual growth.
   Lord, hear us.

5. That those who have passed away may come to experience the fullness of God's love in the Risen Christ.
   Lord, hear us.

Heavenly Father, fill our hearts with courage and hope so that we may be inspired by the example of Peter to labour for the spread of your kingdom on earth. We make our prayer through Christ, our Lord. Amen.

4th Sunday of Easter

First Reading: Acts 13:14, 43-52;
Second Reading: Rev 7:9, 14-17; Gospel: John 19:27-30

Shepherding in the Middle East is a way of life that has changed little from the time of Christ. The popular romantic image of the shepherd guarding his flock that many of us have is far removed from the reality. Shepherding is a hazardous occupation and a tough backbreaking job. It involves all the risks and dangers that are part of living in the great outdoors with little or no protection from the weather, or from wild animals that roam the hills and inhabit the ravines. While shepherds might have had a place in popular folklore, they were rough country folk at the very bottom of the social ladder with no place of importance in society. Their life was lonely and had more to do with sharing the hardship of animals than with working in the company of people. A typical herd of several hundred sheep wandering the hillside required the competence of a highly skilled pair of hands, to guard them from dangers and protect them from harm. While it is customary for many flocks to share a common night-time shelter during the bleak winter months, in the morning without hesitation they answer the call of their individual master, disentangle and go their separate ways.

The wandering figure of the good shepherd, anxiously tending his flock to the point where he is willing to surrender his life for them, is the image this gospel portrays of Jesus. The people who listened to his preaching were very conscious of the strong bond developed between a shepherd and his sheep and had no problem picturing what he meant. Jesus uses this image to stress the intimacy of the relationship between himself and us. It speaks to the deep places of the heart. His aim is to lead, protect and care for his people. The most consoling truth of all is that none of us will ever be lost because, when we stray onto dangerous pathways, the good shepherd is more than willing to search us out and bring us back. When we are in the depths of despair and feel that we have reached the end of the line and are beyond recovery, his hand is always stretched out lovingly, offering us protection and security. There is nothing he will not sacrifice for the sake of his flock. All this should make us realise how precious we are in his eyes and encourage us to follow him, knowing that he cares for and understands our every need and particular situation. We are assured of a permanent place in his love that continues forever. By following his lead we will reach the pastures of eternal life.

This gospel invites us to make a response to Christ's call to 'Come, follow me.' It is the will of the Good Shepherd that we follow his lead and play our part in helping him to build up his kingdom on earth. This may involve a call to change our way of life and a letting go of past values. At home and at work there is no shortage of ordinary people whose lives and example give valuable testimony to their faith. The fruit of their endeavour is found in the caring and rearing of their families and in the compassion they show towards the poor and the elderly. We see this also in the unfailing love of parents who never give up caring for their wayward children and who in spite of many disappointments keep on hoping. In so doing they preach the central message of Christianity, which is to love God and to care for your neighbour.

Vocation Sunday speaks of a divine plan unfolding in all of our lives and of the need to put our trust in God who will show us how to co-operate with it. In whatever work we do we have so much to give and so much to receive. As a Christian community we are called to embrace the challenges of the gospel in our daily lives and act in such a way as to make a difference in our world. The best thing we can do for others is to help them discover how best to find God, discover love and search for a way to serve people in their lives. This Easter season is a time to ask where is my life taking me? We need to deepen within us that desire to serve and love God in our lives, and encourage others in the way they feel called to respond to his love.

Prayer of the Faithful

With confidence we now make our prayer to the Father of our Lord Jesus Christ, whose protecting hand is always watching over us.

1. We pray that the leaders of the church may be filled with a spirit of enthusiasm, so as to faithfully and lovingly watch over the flock of Christ.
    Lord, hear us.

2. That the Lord will inspire young men and women to imitate the Good Shepherd's spirit of service and devote their lives to caring for his flock.
    Lord, hear us.

3. For ourselves, that by the example of our lives we will be a sign of peace and unity to those around us.
    Lord, hear us.

4. For the sick, the weak and the wounded, that their suffering may bring them into a deeper union with Christ, the Good Shepherd.
    Lord, hear us.

5. That all those who have died, that Christ the Good Shepherd may lead them safely home.
    Lord, hear us.

God of mercy and compassion, we thank you for the care you lavish on us. Open our hearts to receive the gift of your love. Grant us the grace to praise you all our days through Christ, our Lord. Amen.

5th Sunday of Easter

First Reading: Acts14:21-27;
Second Reading: Rev 21:1-5; Gospel: John 13:31-35

This gospel comes at the final stage in Jesus' earthly mission and is part of his farewell speech, a type of last will and testament. Jesus not only calls his disciples to love but also to a close union of peace, harmony and justice within the community. This is to be the unique hallmark and identifying badge of his followers. 'By the love you have for one another, everyone will know that you are my disciples.' Love is an over used word, which trips all too readily off the tongue and can mean everything or nothing at all. Even though we talk about love all the time, it is easy to be confused about the meaning of love. As most of us get our cues for loving from popular soap operas and magazines we tend to understand it in romantic and sentimental terms of glamour, spotlight and applause. However, when it comes to putting love into practice and showing our love in practical ways, it requires courage and becomes that little bit more challenging. Many of the causes of pain and suffering in everyday life come from an absence of love.

The command to 'Love one another as I have loved you' is a very radical call because the love the disciples were to show was to be modelled, not on any ordinary fashion, but was to be based on his love for them. The best way we can understand what the Lord meant by love is to observe love as he lived it. For Jesus' love meant helping, affirming, encouraging others and offering them acceptance and unconditional forgiveness. The whole of his life was an utterance of love that was poured out without self-interest and that was spent without counting the cost. He showed this love in the way he served the poorest of the poor and in accepting death on the cross.

Paul and Barnabas were struggling to build community life, founded on love, as they announced the good news on their missionary journey to Antioch. Scripture says that 'they put fresh heart into the disciples encouraging them to persevere in the faith'. Encouragement, it is said, is the oxygen of the soul and without it our enthusiasm dwindles and our commitment slowly starves of appreciation and sometimes dies. Encouragement is something anyone can give and everyone needs. A kind word or a compliment can make dreams and hopes become realities. Those in need of encouragement often feel overwhelmed by the negative forces currently raging in their lives. We know from our own experience that when we are down and feeling low, the bad always seems worse than it is. At such a moment, to have someone point out the good and hold up the positive gives our morale a boost and lifts our spirits. All that it takes to set things in motion is a kind word or a small deed and the best time to start is now. The one thing we need to do is to rediscover the power of love that Jesus preached, for it is life giving and hope fulfilling.

When a close friend or family member dies unexpectedly we are swamped with regret for the things we never said and for the words of appreciation we never got around to expressing. I wonder how many people in our own home are longing to hear a word of praise or commendation that gives hope and is long overdue. We let our children down when we don't tell them how much we love them and how blessed we are to have them. It goes without saying that there is ample room to put love into practice within our own family circle. What is true of the home is true of the workplace and of social life. There are many others who bless us on a regular basis and whose contributions to our life are important. These special individuals are the people we work with and the people who in one way or another make our life so much easier. It is part of our nature to need a sense of belonging not just to a place but to a group of people in whose company we can feel at ease and on whose support we can depend in times of crisis. It is a real privilege to remind them that they are needed, appreciated and valued. A word of encouragement is a rare commodity that costs nothing but goes a long way. We all need it. Why can't we all give it?

Prayer of the Faithful

United by the commandment of love, we present our many needs to the Father in the sure and certain confidence of being heard.

1. For the leaders of the church: may they put fresh heart into their struggle to establish justice and peace in the world.
   Lord, hear us.

2. For ourselves, that we may never be discouraged by our own failures and may our love for one another be sincere, generous and unselfish.
   Lord, hear us.

3. That in all circumstances of life we may show kindness and remain faithful to Christ's new commandment of love, even when those around display hatred and make life difficult for us.
   Lord, hear us.

4. That those who are sick, lonely and depressed may not be discouraged by their pain and suffering but find comfort and hope in those who care for them.
   Lord, hear us.

5. We remember those who have died and also those who have lost a partner through death.
   Lord, hear us.

God of tenderness and mercy, you have given us a wonderful example of love in your son Jesus. Heal the divisions in our families, among our friends and between the churches. Bless us with your care as we make these prayers through the same Jesus Christ, our Lord. Amen.

6th Sunday of Easter

First Reading: Acts 15:1-2, 22-29;
Second Reading: Rev 21:10-14, 22-23; Gospel: John 14: 23-29

No Christian community has ever been without its problems
and there is nothing new about tension and disagreement in the
life of the church. I say this because some of us imagine that the
members of the early church were good holy people who said
their prayers and lived in harmony and peace, and that somehow in later centuries standards slipped resulting in the confusion of our present times. However, rows and divisions have
been there from the very beginning. The first reading describes
such a humdinger of a problem facing the early church as it
grew and extended its boundaries beyond Jewish cultural influence. It concerned the admission of Gentiles into the new community of Christ and had it not been handled properly would
have become an explosive issue and caused a major split. The
conflict was over how a Jewish Christian community should
treat non-Jewish newcomers. How should they relate to one
another? Should the customs of those who first formed the community be imposed on everyone? The burning issue was
whether new arrivals to Christianity would have to follow
Jewish customs including circumcision. The implications of this
would be far reaching for the future of the church. It would
mean that the church would either remain a tiny Jewish sect or
would fling open its doors and embrace people of all nationalities, languages, classes and social groupings, who professed faith
in Jesus Christ. The community leaders made a wise decision in
deciding to discuss the problem rather than smothering the
issue. They knew the difference between argument and dia-
logue and realised that reaching a feasible solution would involve a letting go of some past traditions. While the past is to be
valued, it must not become a hindrance, holding people back
from embracing the present. Having discussed the problem and
prayed about it, once the decision was reached they told the people 'it was decided by the Holy Spirit and ourselves'. Both sides
listened and the Spirit carried the day. The same is true of conflict resolution in our own times. It is important in all decision-

making or solution seeking that we listen to all sides, pray about it and, most importantly, invite the Holy Spirit to guide and direct us, giving him space to do his work.

In the gospel we can sense the natural fear of the disciples when they finally realise that Jesus is leaving them. Jesus was aware of their anxiety and prepared them for his departure with the assurance that they would never be alone. He would always be present in their midst through the action of the Holy Spirit who would teach and guide them. His final words were the pledge of a God-given peace, 'A peace the world cannot give is my gift to you.'

The parting promise of Christ on earth is as relevant today as it was to those frightened disciples. While peace is something we all want, it is good to realise that peace can have varied meanings. For military personnel peace is the absence of war, for a mother it can mean that the children are asleep, for the tired worker, relaxation at the end of an exhausting day. The peace of Christ does not mean that things are going well for us, that we feel happy and content in the knowledge that we have enough to eat, a comfortable home, a family to care for us. The peace of Christ is something deeper and more profound than this. It is a peace that begins with knowing that we are loved and forgiven, that God has seen and experienced the worst of us and has declared his love for us anyway. It means that we are at one with God and in harmony with our neighbour.

Christ invites us all not only to receive his peace but also to share it with those around us. We cannot do this unless we are at ease in each other's company, sympathetic listeners to one another's story, willing to struggle together rather than to pull apart, and when in the wrong to have the humility to say, 'I am sorry.' As human beings, we are a mixture of hopes and fears, strengths and weaknesses and are all wounded to some degree. It is only Christ, through the power of the Holy Spirit who can console us, heal us and bring us peace of mind. However, in order to pass on the peace of Christ we must be at peace with ourselves, all our grudges gone and resentments banished.

Prayer of the Faithful

Aware of God's presence in our midst we make our prayer to renew our faith in his word and our confidence in his church.

1. That the leaders of our church may so live as to be a beacon of light radiating peace and hope to all whom they serve.
   Lord, hear us.

2. We pray that in our families and in our community none of us will saddle our brothers and sisters with burdens they cannot carry or with expectations they cannot meet.
   Lord, hear us.

3. That in a world dominated by wars and rumours of war we may be blessed with the gift of inner peace so as to bring reconciliation in difficult situations and healing where there is strife.
   Lord, hear us.

4. For the sick, the lonely and all those who feel overwhelmed by the pressures of life: may they come to experience Christ's gift of healing love.
   Lord, hear us.

5. For those who have died especially our friends and relatives: that they may be brought into the joyful feast of heaven.
   Lord, hear us.

Heavenly Father, bind us together as your church. Grant us the grace to accept the things we cannot change, the courage to change the things we can and the wisdom to know the difference. We make our prayer through Christ, our Lord. Amen.

Ascension Day
First Reading: Acts 1:1-11;
Second Reading: Ephesians 1:17-23; Gospel: Luke 24: 46-53

Life is busy with entrances and exits – full of arrivals and departures. We are born, we blossom and we fade. People enter the world full of dreams and expectations and leave with tears and sadness. Yet the joy of arriving and the pain of parting help us to get in touch with the Ascension of the Lord, which we celebrate this morning. During the forty days between the resurrection and the Ascension Jesus made several appearances to the apostles, teaching them about the kingdom of God and the responsibilities that lay ahead of them in guiding the church. The apostles are to be his witnesses in spreading the gospel of repentance and forgiveness to the whole world regardless of race or nation. Jesus assured them that although he would be no longer visibly present in their midst, he would remain with them by the power of the Spirit, to the end of time. The apostles for their part have to come to terms with the fact that Jesus will never again walk with them. He has to return to his Father. Having completed his mission on earth and with their responsibilities sufficiently explained, Jesus takes his disciples as far as the outskirts of Bethany, blesses them and is carried up in triumphant glory to heaven. This final separation of the Risen Christ from his disciples crowns his life's work on earth. He who bore our sorrows and shared our sufferings now sits at the right hand of God. The one who had journeyed unto Calvary to make his love known to us and to win our love returns home in triumph to the Father. He is no longer restricted to a particular slice of time or history. The Jesus of earth becomes the Christ of heaven and there begins a new time of witness by those who profess to follow their Risen Lord. It was a happy ending to a period of terrible darkness and self-sacrifice. We are told that the disciples made their way back to Jerusalem with great joy and spent all their time in the temple praising God.

While the Ascension is an ending that rounds off the events of Easter, it is also another beginning. Christ's parting words not only stress the reality of his resurrection but also the urgency of the task that lies ahead of the apostles and the power that will strengthen them. Jesus in the heavens is now and forever part of God. So when Jesus touches the untouchable and loves the unlovable, the Ascension tells us that it is God at work. When Jesus forgives the unforgivable – those who hammered nails into his hands and feet – the Ascension says that it is God doing the forgiving. When Jesus says to a dejected band of disciples that they will be salt of the earth and light for the world, the Ascension says to them and to us that we will inherit his kingdom.

He calls us to witness by our good conduct and kindly deeds to his presence in our lives. This feast is a reminder of the important office that is ours as followers of Christ. We are to continue his work and make his gospel real by our efforts to share in his ministry. He is relying on us to continue to do good in his name. Our mission is to keep his story alive and to preach repentance for the forgiveness of sins so that all mankind may come to knowledge of his infinite love and mercy. Ours is a secular society where religious practice is the exception and not the rule. However, we are earthly vessels in God's divine spark and somewhere at the heart of our Christian faith is the belief and the hope, that the way we live our lives on earth, with the grace of God assisting us, will hasten that day when we will inherit his kingdom. Then the real glory of the created beauty of the world will appear. It will be a world put right, where none are left out or left behind, where good triumphs over evil and where all that is wrong will be made right. It will be a world glimpsed through the life, death and glory of Jesus Christ. However, this will not be realised without a lot of struggle and self-sacrifice, but realised it will be, for the kingdom of God is the meaning of life.

Prayer of the Faithful

On this day of hope and promise, with confidence we make our prayer to the Father, who raised his Son Jesus from the dead who is now seated in glory at his right hand.

1. That the leaders of the church through good and holy lives may bear witness to God's love in the world.
    Lord, hear us.

2. We pray for ourselves that we that we may be mindful of our responsibility for the spread of the gospel by serving the poor and speaking for the voiceless.
    Lord, hear us.

3. For those whose faith has grown dim: we ask the Lord to enlighten them with his word and fill them with his spirit.
    Lord, hear us.

4. We pray for those who are ill and suffering: may the spirit of God come upon them and the comfort of the Risen Lord give them strength.
    Lord, hear us.

5. We pray for the dead: may they experience the joy of Christ's company in heaven.
    Lord, hear us.

Heavenly Father, look upon us with love and help us on our earthly pilgrimage. Enlighten our minds so that we may have a joyous belief in the Risen Christ and so channel his love to others. We make this prayer through the same Christ, our Lord. Amen.

7th Sunday of Easter

First Reading: Acts 7:55-60;
Second Reading: Rev 22:12-14, 16-17, 20; Gospel: John 17:20-26

When we were growing up most of us had colourful dreams of living in an ideal world, where there was peace and perfect harmony and where everybody was the best of friends. Alas such dreams were wishful thinking, as life wasn't like that. Reality always kicked in and wakened us from the slumber of our make-believe world, to grapple with the struggles of everyday living. Nevertheless striving after ideals has its place in life. At the Last Supper Christ placed before his disciples a request that was weighing heavily on his mind. He prayed to his father to grant that his followers would remain one. His earnest desire was that all who professed allegiance to his name would complete the work he had begun. They were to speak with one voice and act as a harmonious community, the united people of God. As Jesus prayed that night for unity he must have foreseen the dreadful harm that a break-off into a multiplicity of denominations would inflict on the church.

This oneness among his followers is an ideal to strive after and we should never settle for anything less. Of all the demands Jesus puts before us in the gospel none is more challenging than this call to unity. He wants all Christians to be animated by love and as united as were the apostles who dined with him at the last supper on the evening before he died. The model of our oneness is nothing less than the unique togetherness that unites God the Father and God the Son. In other words, we are expected to mirror on earth what goes on in heaven. We are to be known for our mutual love and closeness in caring relationships where we share one another's burdens and blessings. Our motto is to be that of the early church, 'See these Christians, how they love one another!' Charity is to be the core of everyone who claims to be a follower of Christ.

A cursory glance at history reveals how far we have all strayed from the unity Jesus prayed for at table with the apostles. Twenty centuries have witnessed quarrels so savage and bitter as to make total reconciliation, humanly speaking an impossible dream. Such bitter feuding and open hostility contradicts the will of Christ 'that they may be completely one'. His request for unity cuts like a razor through the barriers that we have built to keep individuals and groups apart. The damage done to the spreading of the good news of Jesus Christ as Lord and Saviour is enormous. How can we present a clear picture of his message to well-disposed people who are searching for the truth, when we cannot agree among ourselves on what he taught? Many are scandalised and saddened as the church appears to be a house divided against itself, which in the words of scripture must surely fall.

For various reasons we have separate churches and embittered congregations. Most of the divisions have their origins in the corruption, pride and bigotry which, given the right set of circumstances, can spawn hatred and prejudice within any community. Black people can be made to feel uncomfortable as a minority worshipping in a white neighbourhood. Then there are the tensions between liberal interpretations and those who adhere to traditional beliefs. Love of country can be dangerous if it leads people to put the good of their country before loyalty to God's law.

The ecumenical movement, which grew out of a desire to heal the wounds of the past as a first step to complete unity among Christians, is a cause that merits our relentless support. Prayer is the most important source of inspiration in this quest for unity. However, nothing can be achieved if people lack the elementary basics of courtesy and respect for each other as individuals. The good news is that we have made considerable strides in recent years in ecumenical relationships resulting in less animosity and greater friendship among churches. We have become more open and have grown to accept and value each other's tradition as part of the richness of the church. It means we can disagree without being disagreeable. Nevertheless, there does remain a great deal of prejudice that is still deeply entrenched in sectarian strongholds and based largely on ignorance. If this does not bother us, it should. Our love manifested by understanding and tolerance must extend to people of every race and nationality. We who believe in Jesus Christ are called to be architects of reconciliation.

Prayer of the Faithful

Gathered together in hope and in faith like Mary and the apostles awaiting Pentecost, we make our prayer to the Father.

1. We pray that the Holy Spirit may renew the life of the church and make it radiant with hope and joy.
   Lord, hear us.

2. For those who suffer persecution for the sake of the gospel, that they may be courageous in times of trial and show forgiveness to their oppressors.
   Lord, hear us.

3. For a broader vision of life which will enable us to appreciate the differing values and religious traditions within our society so that we can live in spiritual harmony and peace.
   Lord, hear us.

4. For those who are sick, lonely or suffering: may our support remind them of the Father's care and compassion.
   Lord, hear us.

5. That those who have died may know the peace and joy of being with God.
   Lord, hear us.

God our Father, your Son promised to send the Holy Spirit to his apostles. Grant us also an outpouring of your Spirit so that we may be true to your word and faithful to the love you have given us. We make this prayer through Christ, our Lord. Amen.

Pentecost Sunday
First Reading: Acts 2:1-11;
Second Reading: 1 Cor 12:3-7, 12-13; Gospel: John 20:9-23

One of the most painful emotions we have in our makeup is fear.
Our lives are peppered with small fears and sometimes big ones.
Fear is one of the greatest scourges of our age and everyone suffers from it, as it is part and parcel of the human condition. It in-
fluences the development of children, torments young people
and fills the old with insecurity. Fear is a very menacing thing,
and such a widespread experience that we are afraid of something all of the time. We are afraid of disappointing our parents,
failing our exams, being let down, losing our jobs and afraid of
what others might think or say about us. Words like stress, tension, anxiety and worry are part of our everyday vocabulary.
There is nothing wrong with being afraid provided our fear is
reasonable. However, for no given reason fear can come crowd-
ing into our minds, blotting out our happiness, casting its shadow
over everything we do and creating doubt and uncertainty.

In the upper room a group of dispirited followers of Jesus
had gathered and locked themselves in behind closed doors
with fear and insecurity feeding on each other, praying that no
one would discover their hiding place. They were ashamed and
disgraced because of their association with Jesus who was executed as a common criminal. So many of their dreams and expectations had collapsed. Afraid of suffering the same fate as their
master, they were paralysed with shock as they listened for
every step on the stairs, and awaited the knock on the door and
summary execution. Pentecost put an end to such a crippling encounter of fearfulness. With the coming of the Holy Spirit they
experienced something likened to a strong wind and flames of
fire which changed them from a group in hiding, to a courageous band speaking in tongues of the wonderful works of God.

Contrary to all expectations a new sense of their worth was
born. The crowd that gathered to hear them preach in the market place were confused, astonished and amazed as these faint
hearted followers were given a fiery eloquence and filled with
Christ's own spirit. On that day the church started on its journey
and launched out on its mission.

Pentecost calls us to reflect on the part played by the Holy Spirit in our lives. While we are aware of receiving the spirit of the living God in the reception of the sacraments it is important not to fall into the trap of thinking that all the activity of God is confined to these special occasions. Our God is as much a God of the ordinary as of the extraordinary. One does not have to be in a church or among a worshipping community to sense the presence of the spirit at work. God's spirit is no less active and at work in the daily and commonplace happenings of our lives. The realisation of the presence of God can come in an ordinary encounter and fill us with mystery and awe. The Spirit of the living God is equally at work in the home help doing the daily chores for the house-bound members of the local community, when people pop in to check on elderly neighbours, or in the performance of any act of kindness no matter how small. When we are faithful in marriage, sympathetic to the bereaved and supportive to young people, the Spirit of God is active in our midst. If we are prepared to look we can find God in other cultures beyond our own.

Pentecost isn't just a mysterious happening that took place some 2000 years ago at the foundation of the church. It is a deeply personal event calling us to come forward as witnesses on behalf of Jesus. The mighty breath of the first Christian Pentecost is released within us once we open our minds and hearts and invite the Holy Spirit to work within our being. The spirit works wonders wherever human hearts are receptive to its promptings but it is easy to forget this treasure that we all possess, once we lead our lives without prayerful reference to God. As we make our pilgrim journey, obstacles and problems arise which can put us off course and lead us astray if we lack the proper guidance. Amazing things can happen once we allow the Spirit to bring us beyond our own inadequacy. That is why we should pray for the Holy Spirit to fan into flame the dying embers of faith and love in order to mend our broken lives.

Prayer of the Faithful

On this day of Pentecost we pray to the Father for an outpouring of his Spirit into our lives and into the world.

1. We pray for our Holy Father and the leaders of the church. May the Holy Spirit empower them with wisdom and understanding to nourish and guide God's people.
   Lord, hear us.

2. That we may be awakened to our responsibility to spread the gospel wherever we are, so that people may come to know your loving kindness.
   Lord, hear us.

3. For those who find relationships difficult and who feel anxious, isolated or resentful. May the Spirit of peace enable them to be at one with themselves and to reach out in love to others.
   Lord, hear us.

4. For the sick and housebound: may the Holy Spirit comfort them in their suffering and give patience and gentleness to those who care for them.
   Lord, hear us.

5. We pray for those who mourn the death of a loved one: may the Holy Spirit wipe away their tears and turn their sorrow into joy.
   Lord, hear us.

Heavenly Father, we thank you for your countless gifts especially the life you give us in the Holy Spirit. May the love of the Spirit shine in all we say and do. We offer our prayer through Jesus, in the Spirit. Amen.

Trinity Sunday
First Reading: Proverbs 8:22-31;
Second Reading: Romans 5:1-5; Gospel: John 16:12-16

Our Western society is not at all comfortable with the idea of mystery. We like to be in control of our destiny and have an explanation for everything that happens. However, where mysteries are concerned, we can only gaze in wonder. We can know a tremendous amount about people by what they say or do, by their attitude to others or to various situations that they encounter. Nevertheless, there is always more to learn about them and there are always things about them and ourselves that we can never know or fully understand, for at the deep core of every human being is mystery. A real mystery is not something that given certain clues, we will be able to solve and understand. Neither is it completely unintelligible just because there are aspects of it which are completely beyond human understanding. God, however, is the greatest mystery of all and we can only get to understand him in so far as he chooses to reveal himself to us.

This morning we have the first of the great feasts of the church, in which the Trinity, a mystery of faith, gives us a wonderful insight into the life of God. The God of love is around, beside, within and closer to us than we are to ourselves. From the very beginning of the church, the truth of the Holy Trinity has been the central mystery of its living faith and of Christian life. People were baptised into the church, in the name of the Father and of the Son and of the Holy Spirit, to fulfil the command of Jesus to 'Go and make disciples of all nations.' The apostles were in his company when he talked to his Father in heaven using the familiar and affectionate term 'Abba', referred to himself as Son and mentioned going back to heaven in order to send us the Holy Spirit.

We could say that Trinity Sunday is a feast that draws back the curtains on God's life and lets us have a look inside. What we see is that God is a family of three persons – Father, Son and Spirit – bound together in a relationship of love and harmony. We would never have known this had not Jesus Christ told us so, and his word is true. Without the teaching of Jesus we would be left fumbling in the dark and hardly knowing anything at all about God. By watching Jesus in action we learn about God's compassion, forgiveness and love. We also learn that our divine guests invite us to enter their presence, share their company and be part of their life. We believe that Christ brought us into this life of God when we were baptised. He told us that God made us to love and serve him in this world and be happy in his company in the next.

Today's gospel excerpt from John implies that three persons are in the one God but we have no idea how this can be. The creator of all things is totally beyond our comprehension and is a mystery that no one can unravel as it is too deep for words and completely beyond our grasp. However, we can see the blessings the Trinity has showered on the world for which we give thanks. We are left with the truth that God is always greater than our words can express. The mystery of the Trinity is not something we can work out intellectually but it is something to be lived out in our lives.

A famous saying from the early church states that 'God is closer to us than we are to ourselves.' Why is it then that we often feel that there is an immense gulf separating us from him? Perhaps we need to review our relationships with the very source of our life and being. In this way we can evaluate how well we fulfil the destiny our creator has designed for us. Trinity Sunday is a time for reflecting on the presence of God in our midst, in the happenings of our own lives as well as in the people we meet on a daily basis, because that is where God is to be found. Life is by no means plain sailing and we often find ourselves broken and crushed by circumstances. God speaks to us in the sadness and in the distress that come our way. Often we go searching for him in the spectacular while all the time he is to be encountered in the ordinary. We are made in the image and likeness of God and his resemblance is mirrored in our nature and engraved in our hearts.

Prayer of the faithful

Prompted by the Holy Spirit dwelling within us, we confidently approach the God and Father of our Lord Jesus Christ for all our needs.

1. We pray that our Holy Father will discern new directions for our church which will reveal even more clearly in a changing world God's love for humankind.
   Lord, hear us.

2. That through the gift of the Spirit, all Christians may gain a deeper knowledge and understanding of Jesus Christ and endeavour to model their lives on his.
   Lord, hear us.

3. May we develop an appreciation and reverence for the beauty of God's creation and a realisation that we are stewards and not masters of the environment in which we live.
   Lord, hear us.

4. For our young people who are busy with examinations. May the Lord bless and inspire them in their work.
   Lord, hear us.

5. For those who are sick, housebound or unwell: may the Lord bring them hope in times of despair, light in times of darkness and peace when they are troubled.
   Lord, hear us.

6. That those who have died may be brought swiftly into God's glory so that they may see him as he really is and come to enjoy eternal glory.
   Lord, hear us.

Father of heaven and earth, hear the prayers of our wayward hearts. May we always experience your presence among us and continue to be guided by your Spirit. We make our prayer through Christ, our Lord. Amen.

Feast of the Body and Blood of Christ

First Reading: Genesis 14:18-20;
Second Reading: 1 Cor 11:23-26; Gospel: Luke 9:11-17

After a long day of preaching to the multitude about the kingdom of God and healing the sick, Jesus and his disciples were
hungry, exhausted and in need of rest. Furthermore, as dusk
was approaching the apostles were concerned that the crowd,
which showed no signs of dispersing, was without food. When
the apostles asked Jesus to send them off in search of provisions
and lodgings they were surprised at his response, 'Give them
something to eat yourselves,' because the only food at hand was
five loaves and two fishes. Among so many it seemed insignificant but Jesus took the little that was on offer and miraculously
created a meal that more than satisfied the hunger of the multitude. So generous was his act of compassion that when the meal
was finished there were twelve baskets of leftovers.

We, who take our daily bread for granted, are given an insight into the concern the Jesus of the gospel has for sharing food
with the hungry of the world. He wants us to do the same. When
we clothe the naked, shelter the homeless, welcome the stranger
and provide food for the hungry we follow the example of Jesus
and take part in his life's mission. Sharing what we have with
others is not as easy as it sounds because when we become
aware of the enormity of the world's problems and look at our
own meagre resources what we have to offer seems so trivial.
The hunger of people is so vast and our ability so small we may
well wonder what can we do as mere individuals. Since none of
us has all the answers, it is easier to decide not to bother and do
nothing. In this gospel, Jesus is stressing the importance of sharing our bread with the hungry, telling us that our small contribution can make a difference in people's lives and that now is
the time for a new creativity in charity. The promise of the
gospel is that if we share our possessions we will inherit the
kingdom prepared for us from the beginning of the world.

While food satisfies our physical hunger by keeping us alive
and enabling us to maintain a healthy body, breaking bread is
also a sign of our union with each other and a way of bringing

people closer together. A very central part of Christ's ministry took place over meals. Throughout the gospels we learn that Jesus enjoyed gatherings and meals and always sought fellowship with other people. Meal sharing satisfies that deep human need within all of us for intimacy, companionship and community. Many of the miracles of Jesus, like the wedding feast of Cana where he changed water into wine, revolved around food. There are several examples in the gospels of Jesus eating with sinners and tax collectors in their homes. The lives of men like Zaccheus and Levi were changed over these meals. We also see Jesus including meals in his parables and stories, like the anointing at Bethany in Simon's house and the feast prepared for the Prodigal Son on his return home. When people's physical hunger was taken care of over a meal, Jesus gave them added food for thought by making them aware of who he was and stating that he had come from heaven on a life-giving mission. He was the bread of life and would satisfy the deepest hungers of the human heart for hope, meaning, acceptance and everlasting love.

We read at Mass this morning how at the Last Supper on Holy Thursday, the evening of his departure, towards the end of the meal Jesus offered himself as food and drink. He took bread and wine blessed them and passed them around the apostles and told them to 'Do this in memory of me.' He left us a living memorial of himself in the sacramental presence of his body and blood. This desire to be part of our very being in soul and body expresses love at its most intimate. The heart of the matter is that at Holy Communion we are members of God's family gathered around a common table and our Lord nourishes us and becomes food for our souls. God, who is all-powerful, could not have given us a greater gift than that of his Son in the Eucharist as food for our pilgrim journey through life. It is a day for giving thanks to Jesus who gave of himself for all who hunger and thirst for the presence of God.

Prayer of the faithful

Filled with a deep sense of gratitude and joy at the great gift given to us in the Eucharist, we approach our heavenly Father with our requests.

1. For our Holy Father and all called to minister the Eucharist. May the peace of Christ find a home in their hearts so that they may live by the mystery they share with others.
    Lord, hear us.

2. We pray for all those young people who, at this time of year, are receiving Jesus in Holy Communion for the first time: may the Lord keep them in his love and may they find joy in his presence.
    Lord, hear us.

3. We pray for ourselves: may the sharing of the one bread in the Eucharist form us into a community of love were those who are lonely may find comfort and those who are lost may find guidance.
    Lord, hear us.

4. For the sick, the housebound and those who are suffering: may they experience the healing power of Jesus in the Eucharist.
    Lord, hear us.

5. We pray for all those who have died in the peace of Christ. May they rejoice in the eternal banquet prepared for them from the foundation of the world.
    Lord, hear us

Heavenly Father, keep us true to our faith. Inflame our hearts so that we may always recognise you in the breaking of bread. Who live and reign with the Father and the Holy Spirit, one God, forever and ever. Amen.

2nd Sunday in Ordinary Time

First Reading: Isaiah 62:1-5;
Second Reading: Cor 12:4-11; Gospel: John 2: 1-12

At one time or another in our lives, we have all been guests at a wedding. It is amazing to see how different they can be. Some are grand and impressive with coaches and limousines, while others are appealing because of their simplicity. For the newly weds, it is a celebration of great hope and expectation as they pledge their love to each other and promise to become one in mind and heart and soul. Weddings for the Israelites of old were events of enormous social importance, not just for the immediate family but for the whole village. It was one of those rare occasions when families put their best foot forward, placed themselves in the limelight and made a statement about their social standing in the local community. The festivities might last for a whole week and were a time of rejoicing not just for the extended family but for the entire neighbourhood. The wedding feast at Cana is a well-known gospel passage with which we are all familiar and it has embarrassed preachers of temperance for centuries. Indeed there may be some strict teetotalers in our midst who would feel somewhat more at their ease had Christ changed wine into water and not water into wine. Nevertheless this wedding feast provides a fitting setting for Jesus to work the first of his seven signs. It is significant that through Mary's sensitivity a huge source of embarrassment for the newly weds is averted and the happiness of their wedding day is unspoiled. She was the first to notice that the wine had run out and was not going to let the unthinkable happen. Being aware of what was at stake she discreetly approached Jesus to save the situation. His reaction to his mother's plea 'They have no wine' seems somewhat cool if not a sharp rebuke, as if to say he is no longer at her beck and call. 'Woman, why turn to me, my hour has not yet come.' However, when the servants heeded Mary's request to do whatever he asks, the impossible happened and with the marvellous intervention of Jesus, the stone water jars became giant carafes overflowing with the finest of wine. The sight of this must have amazed the onlookers and waiters alike. But only the disciples were aware of what really had happened. With a touch of his divine power Christ blessed the young couple in a strikingly visible way and got their married life off to a good start. The water that became wine signalled the beginning of Jesus' public ministry and revealed he was truly the Lord.

As Christians we must not merely dwell on the wonder involved in changing water into wine. The gospel is a marvellous picture of the loving relationship we have with Jesus who is present in the various activities of our lives. He is aware that our best efforts require the touch of God and is always willing to help especially when we experience difficulties. He brings healing where there is hurt, forgiveness where there is misunderstanding and encouragement where there is a lack of support. The wine is the life of God brought to people through Jesus. He can transform us, taking the ordinary in us and making it extraordinary, turning anguish into wonder and want into wealth. Life is always changed for the better when we allow Jesus into our hearts and home for he enriches the very ordinary, makes it precious and gives an eternal flavour to the commonplace. His presence among us prompts us to think about the shortages in our own lives. Perhaps the glitter has gone out of life? Gone are our dreams and we have settled for the monotony of humdrum routine. Could it be true that we no longer have a zest for living, that we take each other for granted because the sparkle has gone out of our marriage? The gospel is an indication that the richness displayed at the wedding feast of Cana is available to all who call upon Jesus for an increase of grace in their lives. How we are to do this is indicated by Mary. What better advice could we give someone in trouble or anxious about their problems than that of Mary to the wine steward: 'Do whatever Jesus tells you.' A friend of mine who struggled for years to beat his problem with alcohol believes in Jesus' personal intervention in his own marriage. He maintains that it was through his wife's devotion to Mary and the power of Christ that he overcame his addiction. Mary always points to her son as the one who can sustain us amidst the difficulties and problems of life. For all who have entered into a personal relationship with Jesus, the best is yet to come.

Prayer of the Faithful

Confident of receiving the same compassion as was shown by Jesus to the newly-weds at Cana in Galilee, we make our prayer to our heavenly Father.

1. We pray that the church throughout the world may enjoy freedom, love and holiness.
   Lord, hear us.

2. Enlighten those who exercise public office in civil society with a strong and unselfish love as they work for the good of all people under their care.
   Lord, hear us.

3. For married couples that, in times of sorrow, hurt and misunderstanding, they may find Christ and experience his gentle and loving presence at work in their lives.
   Lord, hear us.

4. For the sick, the housebound and those living in isolation, that they may be consoled with the love and concern shown by their neighbours.
   Lord, hear us.

5. We pray for our departed brothers and sisters. May Christ receive them into the glory of his heavenly home.
   Lord, hear us.

Heavenly Father, watch over and help us in the great task of announcing the good news of your Son to the world we live in. When our days are numbered bring us to our heavenly wedding feast. We make our prayer through Christ, our Lord. Amen.

3rd Sunday in Ordinary Time
First Reading: Nehemiah 8:2-6, 8-10;
Second Reading: 1 Cor 12:12-30; Gospel: Luke 1:1-4, 4:14-21

As he moved through Galilee the fame of Jesus spread. People marvelled at the demons he had expelled, the sick he had cured and the evil spirits he had cast out. Word filtered back to his hometown of Nazareth of the reputation he was making and the identity he was forging for himself as a wonder worker. It is no surprise then on returning home that friends and neighbours were curious to find out for themselves what the rest of Galilee was raving about. The opportunity arose when as a preacher he was invited on the Sabbath to lead the Synagogue in worship. We can imagine the hush that came over the congregation and how all eyes were fixed on him and all ears eager to listen as he went forward to lead the community in prayer. He picked up the biblical scroll and, moved by the spirit of God, read a passage from the prophet Isaiah about bringing good news to the poor, liberty to captives, sight to the blind and a year of favour from the Lord. It was a type of personal charter outlining his public ministry, which had just begun. The people were taken aback when Jesus laid aside the scroll and said these very words were being fulfilled in their presence. Listening to what Jesus had to say in the synagogue makes us conscious of the keen sense of justice in the early church and the importance it placed on caring for the poor and looking after the socially deprived. To the great shame of our affluent age, this is no longer the case. This was brought home to me last week while passing through a shopping mall. I noticed an old Romanian lady on bended knees at the main entrance. She was begging, and as she sat with her hand outstretched, tears ran down her cheeks. She had a scarf tied over her undyed grey hair and wore a black crossover apron. Her shoes were patched and worn thin but still highly polished. Her whole stance spoke of finding herself in a position of shame but it was also clear from her demeanour that she had no choice. Either that or she was a good actor. The thought struck me that it must take quite a level of desperation to put yourself so openly at the mercy of others. It reminded me of the sheer poverty of her homeland in contrast to the vulgar abundance which surround us. When you come to think about it, that woman's plight is hard to tally with this morning's gospel message about bringing good news to the poor. It makes me realise that we have a long way to go before we can stand up and say that the Lord's year of favour is being fulfilled in our hearing.

While the poor are always with us, in past decades they have stayed well hidden from the better fed. It used to be possible to lead a well regulated middle-class life in a respectable area and to know no more of poverty other than what is read in books. However, the advent of television has ensured that the plight of these people is neither ignored nor forgotten. Pressure groups are quite correct in reminding us that in a world where we talk carelessly of luxury goods and luxury foods, in the bottom layer of society everything becomes a luxury.

We belong to a church whose mission is to bring the gospel message to the poor and freedom to the oppressed. In a very real sense, we all stand under the judgement of God's word which demands a response in the here and now. From listening to its proclamation in church, we can't honestly say that we don't know what God expects from us. While we should rejoice in our gifts and achievements we must not forget the weaker members of our society. We too are called by God and our mission is to be a power for good by living as Christ did and bringing the good news to all we meet and come in contact with. There is no doubt that Jesus felt a special affinity for the poor people of his day. However, coming back to ourselves, a point worth pondering on is: does our behaviour at home, at work or among our friends indicate that the spirit of the Lord is guiding our lives?

Prayer of the Faithful

Conscious of our sinfulness and aware of our spiritual poverty we turn now to God the Father who brings good news to the poor and ask for his favour.

1. For the church: that through its courageous voice the poor and the broken hearted may hear the good news of God's love and care for them.
   Lord, hear us.

2. That the Lord may open the eyes of those who are blinded by materialism and pride to the meaning of the gospel.
   Lord, hear us.

3. Comfort all those saddened by life and whose hearts are broken with disappointment and misfortune.
   Lord, hear us.

4. We ask your blessing and healing love upon the sick and those who are unwell in mind and body.
   Lord, hear us.

5. We pray for the departed especially (N. and N.) that they may find peace in God's presence.
   Lord, hear us.

Lord and Father, you have shown us your love by sending your Son to share our life. Help us always to act with love and be faithful to your Spirit in all we say and do, through Christ, our Lord. Amen.

4th Sunday in Ordinary Time
First Reading: Jeremiah 1:4-5, 17-19;
Second Reading: 1 Cor 12:31-13:13; Gospel: Luke 4:21-30

Reading this gospel of the rejection of Christ by the people in his own home town of Nazareth brings to mind a short story called the 'Great Stone Face' by Nathaniel Hawthorn. It's about the people in a small New England town who waited for the coming of a prophet and holy man who would look like the features of a stone outcropping in a local hillside. They waited for years but no one ever seemed to turn up and the village declined in hope and spirit. One day an old man died and as he was laid out someone noticed that he did look like the face in the hill. He had been with them all the time and they never recognised him until it was too late. The truth is, they had expected the arrival of someone important and never dreamed of finding the holy man embedded in their midst.

Prophets are accepted provided that they come from some-where else. The people of Nazareth did not believe that God could speak through one of their own. He was just a local car-penter's son who had grown up among them and had no formal education as a rabbi. Jesus was far too ordinary and too close to home to be taken seriously. Their begrudgery prevented them from recognising the presence of God in their own community. In their smugness they knew that the Jews were the chosen peo-ple and enjoyed special preference in the heart of God. No won-der then, when Jesus reminded them that God hadn't any favourites, a wave of disbelief swept across the synagogue. They were disturbed by his arrogance, got very upset, responded with fury, hustled him out of the town and tried to throw him over a cliff.

The role of prophecy in the church is not so much picturing what the future will be like as challenging the community to re-main faithful to the law of God. Prophets like Jeremiah, in the first reading, are lonely figures who stand apart from the crowd and land themselves in serious trouble as they speak out courag-eously against oppression and injustice. Usually they suffer be-cause of what they say. Having special insight from God makes them see things differently, allowing them to ask awkward questions. They view what is happening against the backdrop of eternity, under the eyes of the eternal God and sometimes alert people to the future consequence of their evil actions. Prophets are the voice of the voiceless, who comfort the disturbed and disturb the comfortable. They warn us of the danger of going with the flow and the message they preach is that we must not be made over into the image and likeness of the prevailing culture. We all know that it is easier to string along with the crowd than to stand up and be counted. The mob instinct of ganging up to target a vulnerable individual is strong within human nature. Crowds are cruel and are noted for being ruthless. How often to our shame have we remained silent or joined in the chorus as part of the crowd at the coffee break when a demolition job was being executed on someone's character? We knew what we were doing was wrong but the coward in us was afraid to show disapproval for fear of rejection from the gathering. There is not much difference between character assassination and being thrown over a cliff. All that it takes for evil to win through is that good people do nothing.

The readings are a reminder that God's words are always being spoken. We too are called by God to be prophets and are sent into the world in which we live to make his love and mercy known near and far. Through little thoughtful acts of kindness we can present the face of Christ to an ofttimes uncaring world. The ancient Jewish mystics taught that God is hiding in our world. The only way to find him is in the lives and hearts of our brothers and sisters. Like the people of Nazareth we may find it difficult to believe that God is speaking to us in the ordinary events of our lives. The challenge is to come to an awareness of God in the little things, in the bits and pieces of our own insignificance. It is in the everyday circumstances of home, workplace and community that we meet God. If we fail to encounter him there, we won't find him at all.

Prayer of the Faithful

Conscious of our dependence on God's kind and fatherly care, we open our needy hearts as we make our prayer before him:

1. That the church may continue to be a fearless voice for truth, justice and freedom for the poor, the weak and the exploited.
   Lord, hear us.

2. For an openness of mind and a putting aside of prejudice and bias so as to become people of goodwill in our dealings with strangers.
   Lord, hear us.

3. We pray for all those who are struggling with their faith, especially those who have lapsed from the practice of their religion and for those who are searching for God.
   Lord, hear us.

4. For the sick, the long-term housebound and those recently out of hospital. May they find comfort and recognise the love of Christ in those caring for them.
   Lord, hear us.

5. For our friends, relations and neighbours who have died, that they may attain everlasting joy in heaven with the Lord.
   Lord, hear us.

Lord God, fill our weakness with your strength. Help us to open our hearts to you. May your Spirit remain always with us and may we never take our faith for granted. We make our prayer through Christ, our Lord. Amen.

5th Sunday in Ordinary Time
First Reading: Isaiah 6:1-8;
Second Reading: 1 Cor 15:1-11; Gospel: Luke 5:1-11

There is something quaint about a lakeside with its fishing boats laden down with nets moored in shallow water. Such was the setting for this gospel story at Gennesaret, a heavily populated area at the north-west corner of the lake known as the Sea of Galilee which is rich with an abundance of fish. Those who have an interest in fishing know only too well the frustration Peter and his companions felt after spending the whole night on the water with nothing to show for all their efforts. They were in a depressed mood as they faced back to the lakeshore and settled down to the dreary task of cleaning their nets. Their livelihood depended on a good haul. The command of Jesus to launch out into the deep and cast their nets for a catch was stretching patience and credibility to the limits. Fishermen's work demands great skill as well as a knowledge of the sea and sky. They know the waste of time it is to pay out a net in broad daylight as fish only come to feed on the surface during the night. However, there was something about the personality of Jesus which convinced Peter that this directive was worth a try. There was complete astonishment in his eyes as he sat there gaping at the nets bulging with fish. The sheer quantity of the haul split the nets open and threatened to sink their boat. Peter took a risk, which made all the difference and as a result realised he was in the presence of someone who was more than a man. He was left to face his own self and all he saw was his own sinful unworthiness. His reaction was to get down on his knees and say, 'Leave me Lord, I am a sinful man.'

Ignoring the remark about being a sinner, Jesus invited Peter and his friends to abandon their boats and nets and join him in his mission, his new venture to seek out and save the lost. When they finally reached the shore they beached their boats and without a second thought set off on a vocation that would bring them to a way of life beyond their expectations and desires.

The connecting point between this morning's readings is that the central figure in each is called by God to deliver his message.

Moreover, all three recognise their sinfulness and how unworthy they are to be in the presence of the all-holy God. Isaiah calls himself a man of unclean lips and in a wretched state. Paul reminds us that he is the least of the apostles and to his shame he once persecuted the church of God. Peter realises that he is not fit company for the Lord. However, all are changed by their encounter with God's saving grace.

As members of the body of Christ, God chooses all of us to be bearers of his word and we must always be ready to respond to that call. Few of us will be instructed to teach and preach as was Isaiah, but we are invited to reflect his glory and witness in a less conspicuous way in the ordinariness of life. Whereas Peter was summoned to leave his nets and launch out into the deep, our call to personal holiness is more likely to come as we wash the dishes, help children with their homework, nurse a sick neighbour or look after an elderly parent. What is important is that we respond willingly.

God calls us in many different ways to varied vocations in life. It isn't always easy to accept what we are called to do and to respond to the Lord with a generous heart. Our talents are best used in our local community where we are the voice for the voiceless as we try in our own insignificant way to make things better. As we search for his presence in the world, we all have moments of not feeling up to the job and of being disconcerted by our own inadequacy. Few of us pass through life without feeling the pain of failure. We are all the walking wounded. Some wounds are visible; most are invisible but they are no less real. There are times in all our lives when we become painfully aware of our own sinfulness and the vast abyss separating us from the holiness of God. However unworthy we may consider ourselves, once we realise our need for a redeemer, the forgiveness of God is always there for the asking.

Prayer of the Faithful

Undeterred by our unworthiness, we ask God to purify our hearts as he purified the lips of the prophet Isaiah and so we make our prayer.

1. We pray for our Holy Father and all who have been called to be fishers of men, that they may be filled with inspiration and maintain an enthusiasm for spreading the word of God.
   Lord, hear us.

2. We remember all who work at night, fishermen at sea, staff in hospitals and all who provide a nightly service for their community.
   Lord, hear us.

3. For those whose life is held back and burdened by an inferiority complex and low self-esteem, that they may find confidence, acceptance and self-belief.
   Lord, hear us.

4. For the sick and suffering, that they may discover the presence of Jesus in their pain and confusion.
   Lord, hear us.

5. We remember the dead especially those who have no one to pray for them. May they now enjoy the vision of the Risen Lord.
   Lord, hear us.

Heavenly Father, pour out the healing power of your Son's forgiveness into the shadowy side of our lives as we strive to do your will and bring your word to those around us. We make our prayer through Christ, our Lord. Amen.

6th Sunday in Ordinary Time
First Reading: Jeremiah 17:5-8;
Second Reading: 1 Cor 15:12, 16-20; Gospel: Luke 6:17, 20-26

As we view life from the vantage point of the twenty first century, the one thing we have got to admit is that we have never had it so good. Never in history have we had so much freedom and affluence, so much diversity and choice, as we enjoy today. Come to think of it, the ordinary shopper in the average supermarket is confronted with a display of goods that a century ago would have been beyond the wildest dreams of the wealthiest monarch. Journeys, which a lifetime ago would have taken months, now take less than a day. Ours is the age of space probes to the most distant planets, of capturing on camera the birth of galaxies, of exploring the origins of the universe and of decoding the DNA system of life itself. The frontiers of human progress seem limitless. However, although we have achieved the instant satisfaction of desires, there still is no answer to our oldest dream. Happiness has still proved elusive.

The way we define happiness tells us who we are and in what culture we live. We are painfully aware that in our consumer dominated society, riches and possessions are held up as an indispensable avenue to happiness and all that we need for a prosperous life. At the same time appearances are deceptive, for if wealth brought happiness then every wealthy person should be happy. We often notice that what seems like an individual's success story, for all its comfort and security, doesn't necessarily bring happiness. The route to happiness turns out to be harder than taking the waiting out of wanting. We do not find happiness in the pursuit of pleasure or in the satisfaction of desire. They can never deliver our deepest hopes and longings.

There is little doubt that something has gone wrong among the many beautiful things that we have in today's world. While we are going at breakneck speed in the pursuit of progress, we are not quite sure where we are going and are in danger of losing the plot. The human story is one of continuous advance but survey after survey shows that we are no happier than our parents were a generation ago, and our children are even less so. Happiness is less about what we possess than the good we do.

The Beatitudes, those memorable sayings of Jesus, show how sharp the contrast is between the common perception of what it means to be happy and what true happiness is. When we first hear them, their reasoning seems totally absurd as they contradict the received wisdom of the age. However, we are not living in a perfect world and the way things are is not necessarily the way they should be. We are familiar with the saying that God's ways are not our ways and the beatitudes give us a glimpse of the way God looks at things. They are a strong statement that his view of success and failure, joy and sorrow, want and plenty is different from ours. By presenting us with a bigger picture and broader horizon of life, they make us realise that what we possess in this world is of fleeting significance and something that will pass away. The essence of the Christian message is that Jesus sees things differently than we do and his values stand in sharp contrast as to what the world holds important. Holiness and wealth do not fit comfortably side by side. Human success and power count for nothing in God's eyes. What Jesus proposes is that we live by gospel values and not by our own natural impulses.

This gospel does not set out to make us feel comfortable. We cannot hear it without reflecting where our hearts are and where our values are rooted. While we cannot live without money the Beatitudes caution us about the pursuit of selfishness, which makes us feel empty and stale inside. Something we must all dwell on is whether we are putting down roots in material status or human kindness. Which of these is of greater importance to us? One of the paradoxes of life is that we can encounter happiness and peace of mind when we are more concerned about other people than we are about ourselves. Basing our lives upon the beatitudes is not an easy option and few of those who do it will ever attain worldly importance. But the reward is an inner joy that no one can take away.

Prayer of the Faithful

Aware of the danger arising from putting our trust in the pleasures of this world, we lift up our hearts in fervent prayer to the Father.

1. We pray that the church throughout the world may preach and foster true justice for the poor and the oppressed.
   Lord, hear us.

2. Help us to discover that we become truly rich and pleasing in the eyes of God not by receiving but by serving and giving to others.
   Lord, hear us.

3. We pray for our young people. May they persevere in the pursuit of their ideals and never be discouraged by failure.
   Lord, hear us.

4. For those whose love is unsung – parents of children with special needs, those who care for aged parents and all those bearing silent witness to the love of God in their suffering at home or in hospital.
   Lord, hear us.

5. For the dead, that they may they see the Lord in whom they trusted face to face.
   Lord, hear us.

God our Father, through the teaching of your Son, you have made known the blessing of your kingdom. Help us to see, with the eyes of faith, the truly important things of life and give us the courage to live them. We make our prayer through Christ, our Lord. Amen.

7th Sunday in Ordinary Time
First Reading: 1 Samuel 25:2, 7-9, 12-13, 22-23;
Second Reading: 1 Cor 15:45-49; Gospel: Luke 6:27-38

The religious leaders in Jesus' time had a law which said, 'an eye for an eye and a tooth for a tooth', and the expectation was to strike back at those who harmed them in any way. The words spoken by Jesus in this morning's gospel, 'Love your enemies, do good to those who hate you, bless those who curse you and pray for those who treat you badly', may sound as disappointing to us as they did to the disciples. Instead of wanting to destroy our enemies, as was the popular belief in Old Testament times, we are called to go beyond what would ordinarily be expected and love them in an extraordinary way. Such behaviour illustrates the extremes to which, as followers of Christ, we must be willing to go in order to be merciful, as God is merciful. We are called to look at ourselves and break free from the tit for tat cycle of recrimination by meeting hatred and violence with love. In this way we witness to the heavenly Father whose image we reflect.

It would be hard to find another passage in the bible that is so much at odds with our customary way of treating people. This extraordinary reversal of the usual manner of doing things is contrary to what we have come to feel and believe. We live in a world where getting even and levelling the score is raised to the level of a virtue. It goes against the grain to part with possessions, to give to everyone who asks without expecting payment or refuse to pass judgement on anyone. Wouldn't our enemies have a field day if we refused to confront them? Try as we may, there are some people we just cannot stand and dealing with them is one of the ongoing challenges of daily life. We have only got to think of the neighbour who pesters us, the person who talks behind our back or plays loud music into the dead of night.

It is true that we have all experienced our fair share of hurts in life and have wasted endless energy trying to settle old scores. One of the most difficult lessons to learn is forgiveness of those who have wronged us. The reluctance to forgive and the rush to judgement is the kind of thing that Jesus is trying to eliminate from our lives, and he sets the example for us through his own life as he extended the hand of love, kindness and forgiveness until his death on the cross when he prayed, 'Father, forgive them.' He never sought revenge or retaliation against those who wanted to hurt him and in the end it cost him his life. Forgiveness is a life-giving force that checks the downward spiral of hatred and revenge. The whole story of salvation is one of loving forgiveness. If we don't want to be fixed in an attitude of unending retribution, there is no alternative to living on the basis of the Lord's Prayer. Every time we recite The Lord's Prayer our request for forgiveness is conditional on ourselves showing forgiveness to those who have offended us. Not to forgive is to harbour resentment and to allow enemies to have control over us.

In the gospel we are being called to a radical new pattern of human conduct and invited to model our behaviour on the life of Jesus who urges us to be compassionate as is our heavenly Father. Compassionate people are essentially givers of their time, possessions, sympathy and support. No matter where we are or in what situation we find ourselves, hardly a day goes by that does not afford us an opportunity of putting compassion into practice. There is more to compassion than a tear in the eye, a sentimental tug of the heart or a passing feeling. Compassion prompts us to let go of our fears, to be generous with our forgiveness and allow God to take control of our lives. It involves entering into another's pain no matter how desperate, shocking and wretched the situation may be. It means that we avoid being judgemental as each of us is a sinner and none of us knows how any person stands before God. Our generous compassion is a reflection of God's unbounded love for us. Christianity is essentially a religion of love and people who love do things differently. They live by a different set of values for they truly believe that there is more joy in giving than in receiving. They have no difficulty in showing their love without expecting something in return as they have learned to love with the all-embracing love of Christ.

Prayer of the Faithful

Called by Christ to imitate the compassion and love of our heavenly Father, who is slow to anger and rich in mercy, we make our prayer.

1. We pray for the leaders of the church. May they carry out their mission of spreading the good news kindly, gently and with love.
   Lord, hear us.

2. Fill our lives with an awareness of your loving care for those who are weak and give us the courage to do what we can to help them.
   Lord, hear us.

3. We pray for families that are torn apart with dissension and unhappiness, that they find peace and reconciliation.
   Lord, hear us.

4. May the Lord in his mercy be close to the sick, the dying and those who carry heavy burdens.
   Lord, hear us.

5. For those who have died, especially N and N, that they may know peace and find rest in the kingdom of God.
   Lord, hear us.

Heavenly Father, help us to love others as you love them. May all the actions of our lives bear witness to your mercy and goodness. We make our prayer through Christ, our Lord. Amen

8th Sunday in Ordinary Time

First Reading: Ecclesiasticus 27:4-7;
Second Reading: 1 Cor 15:54-58; Gospel: Luke 6:39-45

The songwriter F. R. David was struggling to put his feelings into words and, finding it easier to express himself in song, he wrote a hit number some years back called 'Words don't come easy to me'. I am not going to break forth into song but I have been struck recently by the great human faculty of speech, which we use to communicate a vast range of things to each other. Words give us great emotional release as they enable us to tell someone else about our feelings and ideas. However, they often fail us and leave us speechless as we struggle to communicate peak moments of joy and anger, love and sorrow. At times like this we are dumbfounded and reduced to silence.

Words are endowed with an extraordinary power for good or for evil, to encourage or to frighten. We can use words to build up people, to express gratitude, to thank friends but they can also be used to knock neighbours, insult family and cause division within a community. A kind word heals and a cruel word hurts. Not everything we think is something we should say. Words are a powerful expression of what we are and who we are because they shape our being. At times we might be inclined to say, 'It is only a word.' However, once spoken, we can never take back our words. It goes without saying that we reach an all time low when we resort to the use of bad language. Foul-mouthed vulgarity does untold harm to our ability to be civilised and to relate gently to each other. Let's remember that as Christians we have a special responsibility to use our words to spread the word of God on earth.

Jesus was a craftsman with words, drawing images, painting parables with simple words, speaking to those areas of the human heart which cope with guilt, forgiveness and acceptance. People who listened to him speak were astonished at the gracious words that flowed from his lips. He used language fabulously to tell us about love and forgiveness, about compassion and the beauty of God at the heart of all creation. There was never any contradiction between what he said and what he did.

In today's readings, which are a series of sayings, he invites us to be radically honest when we ask ourselves, 'What sort of a person am I, what is the fruit of my life, what effect do I have on others and how do I use my words?' These are all challenging questions and to answer them honestly is even more challenging because we might just see in ourselves something that we really don't like. There is a shadow side to all of us that we would rather keep to ourselves. We hide behind masks because our capacity for self deception is quite remarkable. What you see is often not what you get. Jesus describes as hypocrites those who notice faults in others, but who are blind to their own shortcomings. We are all guilty of hypocrisy when we put down others for the very faults we have ourselves. Engaging in gossip about a friend, complaining about theft in the workplace when we have lined our own pockets or becoming upset when a promise has not been fulfilled while we regularly renege on our pledge, are just some of the occasions when we are hypocritical. We are all good at picking holes in other people's character and behaviour while forgetting about our own shortcomings. The truth is that while we pride ourselves on our balanced outlook and on having a sharp eye for noticing things, we often are blind to seeing ourselves as we really are.

Christ is asking us to face ourselves with courage and honesty before we take a look at those around us with whom we find fault. Jesus was never in the business of judging. It may be helpful to remember that when we point the finger at someone in judgement three other fingers from our own hand are pointing back at us. If only we could see ourselves as others see us.

We are all on this earth together, doing the best we can. Since we never know the pain and struggle others may be experiencing, we are ill equipped to act as their judge. In this regard the Sioux Indians have a very apt saying: 'Great Spirit, help me never to judge another until I have walked in his moccasins.' As followers of Christ we must be people of integrity and avoid being judgemental.

Prayer of the Faithful

Prompted by the spirit we open our hearts to the God of grace, confident that he will hear our prayer.

1. We pray for our Holy Father, that the Lord may grant him wisdom and courage, to guide and govern the church.
   Lord, hear us.

2. May we always use the wonderful gift of speech to praise and thank God and to comfort and encourage our neighbour.
   Lord, hear us.

3. For the ability to look into our hearts, see our faults and refrain from passing comment on the shortcomings of others.
   Lord, hear us.

4. We pray for the sick, the sorrowing and those troubled in mind or body. May the Lord touch their lives with his healing power.
   Lord, hear us.

5. We remember the dead and all those who grieve for their loved ones. We pray that God may keep them in his love and peace.
   Lord, hear us.

Father, in your gentle mercy guide our wayward hearts for we know that left to ourselves we cannot do your will. We make our prayer through Christ, our Lord. Amen.

9th Sunday in Ordinary Time
First Reading: 1 Kings 8:41-43;
Second Reading: Galatians 1-2, 6-10; Gospel: Luke 7:1-10

The scene presented to us in this gospel passage is one of openness and mutual respect. The centurion, the central figure in the story, is not a Jew or a Christian but a pagan officer of the hated Roman army that was an occupying force in Palestine. As an outsider he represented the oppressors, the foreign government which did not understand local traditions, customs or attitudes. His kind of presence in this land of clannish, narrow-minded people was anything but welcome. Worse still, in a religious sense he was outside the means of salvation as he was a pagan who worshipped idols. However, appearances can be deceptive for he must have been a very humble and compassionate individual who was sympathetic by nature, because he cared deeply for his seriously ill servant. To his credit, he knew the value of building good human relationships at a local level with the Jewish people. Soldiers of his rank and position were persons of authority and things happened as soon as they gave the command. The wisdom of the years had taught him not to place too great a value upon his position as a commander of an outpost of the empire. At a time when it was customary for Romans to treat Jews with disdain and total disrespect, he held them in high esteem. Moreover he was so sympathetic to the Jewish people that he helped out in the construction of their synagogue. Unashamedly he sought the assistance of the Jewish elders and sent them to plead with Jesus to save the life of his dying slave. The humility, reverence and faith of the man was so strong that he believed all Jesus had to do was merely to say the word and his friend would live. He did not feel worthy of the honour of having so holy a man of God come under his roof.

In the light of all this it comes as no surprise that Jesus marvelled at the deep personal faith of the centurion and remarked that he had not found so much faith among the chosen people. One of the most striking features about the officer was that, in a world of inhumanity and superstition, he stood out as a man of compassion and faith. In a world of darkness he stood out like a beacon of light and an example of all those who come to God through faith in Jesus. At each eucharistic celebration, before we receive the body of Christ, we pray the words of the centurion, 'Lord, I am not worthy to receive you, but only say the word and I shall be healed.'

The centurion, standing to attention in the street at Capernaum, is not only the backbone of the Roman army but also a fine example of faith to those who find it impossible to step outside the boundaries of their limited religious horizons. There is nothing narrow, crippled or bigoted about his outlook on life. He is a man who faces and accepts facts with the calm assurance of someone who has placed his problems in the hands of God. By the way he behaves we can see that he realises God's house is open to all – that God has a place for everyone who calls on his name, that there is no such thing as an outsider or a foreigner as far as Jesus is concerned. As he shared his faith with those in the locality, so we are challenged to share ours.

Some of us listening to the story of the Centurion at Capernaum may regard him as a charismatic figure who just happened to come on stream at that time and as a result things worked out smoothly in the neighbourhood. Life doesn't work that way. Good relationships don't just happen but are a hard won achievement and the result of people with vision working hard to attain the goal of living in harmony. The centurion did more than grace Capernaum with his presence. He got involved in the local community, respected their religion, organised the construction of their synagogue, respected people as people and cared especially for those in his employment. That kind of sharing is not always easy and involves a lot of groundwork. It is also a reminder of the way that God is at work sometimes in the people we think are our enemies. The centurion is a model for Christians of all ages in the way his faith focuses attention on God and on how helpless we are without him.

Prayer of the Faithful

We now ask the Lord to make us strong in faith so that, following the example of the centurion, what we say with our lips, we may believe in our hearts and practise in our lives.

1. We pray for the leaders of the church. May they bear witness to the missionary spirit of the gospel in their preaching and teaching, so that those searching for the truth may find true life and peace of soul.
    Lord, hear us.

2. For civic leaders and all those holding positions of authority, that they may be active in good works and guided by justice and truth in all their decisions.
    Lord, hear us.

3. May we play our own small part in the spreading of peace by learning how to make people from other cultures feel welcome in our midst.
    Lord, hear us.

4. We pray for all those who are carrying the cross of suffering: the poor, the sick and the lonely. May they, like the centurion, experience the comfort of God's love.
    Lord, hear us.

5. We pray for those who have died, especially those who have no one left on earth to pray for them: may they rest in peace.
    Lord, hear us.

Heavenly Father, pour your Spirit into our lives. Renew our gift of faith that we may trust in you more fully and accept your will in all things. Make us worthy to receive those blessings for which we ask through Christ, our Lord. Amen.

10th Sunday in Ordinary Time
First Reading: Hosea 6:3-6;
Second Reading: Romans 4:18-25; Gospel: Matthew 9:9-13

In the nature of things we live in a valley of tears and our world is full of broken hearts. This feeling of hopelessness is something we all experience from time to time but especially when we lose a close friend or family member. Death is never kind and leaves us with a sense of emptiness, sadness and loneliness. It happens that while Jesus and his disciples are entering the town of Nain they meet a funeral procession. A poor widow and sorrowing mother is mourning the loss of her only son who is being carried out to the cemetery for burial. That the dead man is young only heightens the tragedy. With his death the unfortunate mother's whole world has collapsed. She has been deprived of the only source of support and comfort in her old age. In the absence of her deceased husband she is bereft of the sole person on whom she can depend. To be a parent in such a situation must be one of the most painful and powerless state of affairs anyone can experience. In the natural order of things, parents are not meant to be standing at a graveside burying their children. This son is all she has. The scene of this tragic event is truly harrowing, so much so that Jesus is moved by the pitiful plight of the grieving widow. His heart goes out to the sorrowing woman who is going through her darkest hour. There are no limits to the healing love of Jesus. Touched by the mother's distress he moves forward, takes control of the situation, tells her not to cry and, acting with concern and sensitivity, restores her son to life. We then learn that the young man sits up immediately and begins to talk.

This soul touching story of restoring life to the dead son of the widow of Nain, is a truly beautiful insight into the heart of Jesus. Witnessing human suffering and seeing people marginalised on the hard shoulder of life touched him deeply. He was always ready to weep with those who weep. The miracle is so public that the whole village realises this to be an awesome happening and beyond their ability to understand. The power of Jesus in restoring life to the dead man is recorded simply and without fuss. We are told that a great fear swept the town's folk who were filled with amazement and conscious of being in the presence of God's healing influence. Many would describe this incident as the most touching story in the four gospels. It portrays a human helplessness which no one but God can relieve. Here we see the tenderness of God reaching out to the sorrowing woman in the person of Jesus Christ.

From time to time in our own lives we all encounter situations of loss similar to this gospel story. These are the emotionally crushing happenings over which we have absolutely no control. Recently I received news that the son of good friends of mine had been involved in a serious car accident. Life instantly changed for them. The things that seemed so important beforehand suddenly paled into insignificance with the gift of life and health hanging delicately in the balance. None of us has the responsibility to care for the whole world. Instead, our task is to care for the people who are closest to us and in need of our help. This gospel shows that it is part of God's plan for us to help ease another's burden by giving of ourselves and entering into their pain with gentle and tender hands. Jesus didn't make it easy for himself by avoiding the widow's troubles, but waded right in and helped out. The friend who cares makes it clear that whatever happens in the outside world, being present to each other in a time of need is what really matters. When accidents or other unfortunate events occur, we get our priorities right as we start to think of the little things of each day that often pass us by without a word of gratitude. Wherever we are on life's journey, Christ's power and compassion can meet us there. Living each day with an awareness of the blessings that we too often take for granted is the proper way to live. It does not prevent the pains and heartaches that life throws at us from coming to our door, but it does keep us close to the peace of God and strengthens our ability to cope with difficulties when they arise.

Prayer of the Faithful

Confident of sharing in the everlasting life won for us by Jesus, we open our hearts to the Father and place our needs before him.

1. We pray for Our Holy Father and the leaders of the church. May they be channels of grace and unerring guides for the people of God.
   Lord, hear us.

2. May we, in our lives, show the same love and compassion that Jesus showed to the widow of Nain, to those who need our help.
   Lord, hear us.

3. For those whose calling is the caring professions, that they may be able to reflect the gentle consolation of the Lord in their ministry.
   Lord, hear us.

4. For those among us who are sick or whose minds are failing, that like the widow's son they may experience the healing hands of Jesus in their suffering.
   Lord, hear us.

5. We remember in our prayers the faithful departed. May they be raised to the fullness of new life in the presence of God.
   Lord, hear us.

God our Father, help us to grow in compassion so as to give hope to the broken hearted. We make our prayer in the name of Jesus the Lord. Amen.

11th Sunday in Ordinary Time
First Reading: 2 Samuel 12:7-10, 13;
Second Reading: Gal 2:16, 19-21; Gospel: Luke 7:36-8:3

Grand social gatherings in the Palestine of the gospels were usually centred around a meal. Jesus was always glad to avail of such opportunities to teach and to preach the good news. When this highly unusual incident takes place he happens to be a guest at table in the house of Simon the Pharisee. A lady of the night who enjoys a certain notoriety in the locality approaches the table and kneels down beside Jesus. Oblivious of propriety, she lets down her hair, covers his feet with kisses and anoints them with a perfumed ointment. Even though she is a sinner she has a deep awareness of the kind of person he is for she comes into his presence with confidence and without fear of being rejected. There is something about him that stirs a profound respect within her and she shows her deference by anointing his feet with precious ointment. Without uttering a word she lays down her burden of guilt at his feet. As she works she sheds tears of thankful appreciation at the enormous relief of being forgiven, accepted and welcomed home with her dignity fully restored. To the onlookers her actions seem strange and extravagant. All of them would have treated her with contempt and as an object of scorn. One question is on all of their lips. If Jesus really is a prophet how can he let this streetwalker touch him? Aware of the shock and horror among the onlookers, Jesus uses the occasion to drive home a message about respect and forgiveness. He confronts his host about the way he sees other people and points out that the sinful woman is closer to God than he is. In fact, the extravagant love of this kerb crawler is preferable to his untouchable welcome. Good manners demand that cool water be poured over a guest's feet on arrival after a dusty journey and to omit it, as Simon does, is an act of discourtesy. Simon fails to recognise Jesus as someone with something special to offer.

The moving encounter between Jesus and the sinful woman in the house of Simon is an indication of God's immense desire that sinners be reconciled to him. It is one of the great examples of repentance and forgiveness that leads to healing. What Jesus

114

is saying is that love covers a multitude of sins. This woman is a lesson on how no one is outside the scope of God's forgiveness. She is an outcast who has found very little happiness in life but has always longed for acceptance from the men who used her body for their own satisfaction. Her sorrow is the key that opens the door to a new life. It is an intense sorrow that drives her to come forward publicly and, in full view of everybody, anoint Christ's feet as a sign of repentance. No matter how terrible the sin, God is ready to look upon it as if it had never been commited. Notwithstanding all that happened to her, she finds a better future in the Lord who restores her dignity. The woman knows that Jesus has forgiven her sins and recognises her as a person in her own right.

What is so wonderful about this gospel is that it places the same unlimited and all embracing forgiveness, which Christ extends to the nameless woman, within the reach of everybody. There is no end to the forgiveness of God. It isn't possible for a person to fall on their knees in the presence of God and not to be forgiven. The only limitations to what the Lord can do in our lives are of our own making. To begin, we have to acknowledge our own wrongdoing and our need for God's mercy and pardon. Once that is done there is nothing to fear from an all-forgiving God. Our sins small or great, few or many, are wiped away by the sheer might of God's great healing love. In our own turn we must be as ready and forgiving to each other as God has been to us. Forgiveness is not just something we receive; we are obliged to share it with those members of family and friends with whom we are at odds. The holding of grudges and the nursing of hatreds take a long time to shake off. The longer they go on the more irreversible they become. For most of us forgiveness is a slow journey. It is so difficult to rid ourselves emotionally of past wrongs. However, to avail of the Lord's forgiveness we have to let go of all bitterness. Otherwise we shall not find pardon and peace. Without forgiveness, we wither and die.

Prayer of the Faithful

We bring our petitions before our gracious, loving and all for-giving Lord who is the source of life, confident that he will listen to our prayers.

1. We pray for the church. May it always remember that it is a channel of our Father's compassionate love and a refuge for sinners, and not a safe haven for the perfect.
   Lord, hear us.

2. May we always imitate the patience, tolerance, and forgive-ness of Christ in our dealings with the weak and vulnerable and those who find themselves on the fringes of society for whatever reason.
   Lord, hear us.

3. For those who are trapped in the habit of sin and burdened with guilt. May they be treated with compassion and experi-ence the healing peace that follows reconciliation with God and neighbour.
   Lord, hear us.

4. We pray for the sick and the lonely. May the Lord comfort them with the strength of his healing love.
   Lord, hear us.

5. We ask the Lord to welcome all our deceased relatives and friends into the everlasting peace of his eternal home.
   Lord, hear us.

Heavenly Father, give us a real and heartfelt sorrow for our sins. Help us to show a sincere spirit of forgiveness to others. May we reach out with joy to grasp your hand and walk in your ways through Christ, our Lord. Amen.

12th Sunday in Ordinary Time

First Reading: Zechariah 12:10-11;
Second Reading: Gal 3:26-29; Gospel: Luke 9:18-24

Every so often the world we inhabit throws up a larger than life personality whose fame spreads far and wide and makes a deep impression on the current scene. What they say and do either causes offence or wins acclamation. It fascinates some people while others are not at all comfortable with the new arrival on the scene. They are critical of their utterances and regard them as disturbers of the peace. Jesus is one such individual. His personality leaps out from the pages of the gospel and as somebody different, gives rise to comment and controversy. He has an outlook on life and a vision of the future that gives people hope. His siding with the poor and the outcast questions in a challenging manner the accepted thinking of the times. Not everyone is comfortable with his appearance in town. All kinds of rumours are afloat as he attracts a band of followers from various walks of life and from every political and social sector of the population. The crowds are curious as to his identity but when Jesus asks his closest followers, 'Who do people say that I am?' nobody gets it right. The guesses all point to someone else – Elijah, John the Baptist or one of the prophets. That is why Peter's spontaneous confession, which recognises the fullness of his personality, must have been a real joy to the ears of Jesus. Peter expresses the faith of all of the apostles. He claims Jesus is Lord in whom all the promises and expectations of old are fulfilled.

While Peter gave the correct answer and used the right words, his profession of faith did not imply a complete understanding of what Jesus' messiahship was all about. He still had a lot to learn. Little did he realise that the life of the Messiah would be bound up in being the suffering servant of God. This would take a long time to sink in as it ran contrary to popular expectations. The disciples' idea of messiahship was linked to power and success, to glory and greatness. They had the mistaken notion that all hardship would be taken away from their lives and they had to learn painfully that the standards of Christ are not those of prosperity and wealth. The greatness, happiness and success that he promised would come, but at a cost. Jesus did not always find it easy to get his message across to the apostles. In spite of all they saw and heard, they were often blind to the real truth. By questioning his apostles about what people thought of him, Jesus opened up a way to teach them the true nature of his mission. He had a destiny to fulfil and that was to accomplish the will of his father. His mission was to restore a shattered world and bind up hearts that were broken. He would redeem humanity by his death and make eternal life possible through his resurrection. None of this would be easy. Jesus made it crystal clear about the high cost involved in being one of his followers and never at any time pretended that it would be less than demanding. He alerted the apostles to the reality that suffering is the blood, sweat and tears of life. At the same time, the cross that is planted at the centre of Christian living is not an invitation to lead a miserable life but is a call to hope in the face of those sufferings, which are a normal part of human existence. We must accept that God's way of doing things runs contrary to our expectations. Our Lord's teaching is for real life and real life can be very difficult.

The question addressed to Peter two thousand years ago, 'Who do you say that I am?' is addressed to us today. This was a determining question for the disciples and it is for us as well. Our salvation depends on our answer. Each of us has to make an individual response. Do we experience Jesus as someone who plays an important part in our daily life? Belief that he is the Christ of God should prompt us to reflect on how prepared we are to follow him. To journey with him, we must take up the cross of daily living so that he can lead us into the fullness of life. Growth in our relationship with Jesus involves a willingness to turn our lives over to him. Genuine disciples have to adopt the convictions, attitudes and values of their master.

Prayer of the Faithful

We place our trust in the creator and Father of humankind who comforts the sorrowful and hears the cries of the afflicted.

1. For the church throughout the world, especially in countries suffering persecution, that through the preaching of the good news, true charity may replace aggression and hatred.
   Lord, hear us

2. We pray for those who courageously proclaim their faith and are suffering for their beliefs. May God sustain them in their trials and as they walk through the valley of darkness may they experience the warmth of his loving support.
   Lord, hear us.

3. For the courage to be willing to make sacrifices, to take up our cross every day and to learn from our failures and disappointments.
   Lord, hear us

4. Give your strength to the sick and bless all those who minister to them with your loving kindness.
   Lord, hear us

5. May those who have died enjoy forever the fullness of God's saving power.
   Lord, hear us.

Lord God, the death of your Son brought life to the world. Help us to follow faithfully in his footsteps and to recognise the cross and suffering not just in the great trials of life but in our daily acts of self-denial. We make this prayer through Christ, our Lord. Amen

13th Sunday in Ordinary Time
First Reading: 1 Kings 19:16, 19-21;
Second Reading: Galatians 5:1, 13-18; Gospel: Luke 9:51-62

Every journey has a measure of the unknown and that was true
for Jesus as he made his way to Jerusalem. Setting off on this
new phase of his ministry, Jesus was aware of the fate that
awaited him. Nevertheless he had hoped to find hospitality in a
Samaritan village and extend the hand of friendship to its people. Once more he experienced misunderstanding and rejection
when the inhabitants closed the gates on him because he was a
pilgrim on the way to the temple. Hostility had smouldered between Samaritans and the Jews for centuries. The Samaritans
had intermarried with foreigners and the Jews considered them
to be religious half-breeds. They were sworn enemies and it was
a risky business for Jews to use this short cut through Samaria
on their journey to Jerusalem to worship. The Samaritans had
their own holy mountain and the temple in Jerusalem represented
all that they hated and despised about the Jews. The reaction of
James and John was predictable. They ask leave to call down the
wrath of God on the Samaritan village as if a touch of fire and
brimstone would put manners on the inhabitants. Christ would
have none of their violence. He refused to have anything to do
with their bigotry, for he had come into this world on a mission
of peace and reconciliation. Anyone wishing to be one of his followers would have to renounce such conduct.

When three young men make an approach hoping to become
his disciples he spells out forcefully what exactly is demanded.
Far from encouraging them to become followers, he entices none
of them into believing that discipleship would be rosy or romantic. Christ dampens the enthusiasm of the first by stating that
following in his footsteps means giving up the comfort and
security of house and home to accompany an itinerant preacher
who has nowhere to lay his head. It will take enormous courage
and resolve to travel along a road that leads to hardship and
trial. The second candidate who is recently bereaved discovers
just how severe these demands are when he is told bluntly 'to let
the dead bury the dead'. Christ's work is with the living and it is

a message of new life in God. He makes it clear to the third prospective applicant that half-hearted loyalty is not enough. Once a decision is made, there can be no turning back. It means following Christ unreservedly and nothing must get in the way of putting him first.

All through our lives God is calling us as he called Elisha who had no second thoughts about following Elijah and accepting the uncompromising office of prophet. He severed his links with the past by slaughtering his oxen and destroying his plough. Likewise, God is constantly calling us out of the cosy existence of our comfort zones, challenging us to live our faith at home among our family, in our work place and in our social life where we mix with friends. Christian commitment is not a Sunday affair and must cover all facets of our lives. Commitment is one of the deepest elements in our experience. We have only got to think of how undermined a partner in marriage feels on discovering that his or her spouse is no longer committed to their relationship or a child who experiences the same lack of confidence and insecurity about a parent. A regrettable aspect of modern life is the fact that commitments are regularly broken. When faced with harsh demands there is a tendency to make excuses and seek an easier and simpler way out. We have no difficulty in giving our word and professing unswerving loyalty to the Christian principle of justice but are soon exposed to compromise. Having a habit of making excuses makes us half hearted and deprives us of the joy and satisfaction that comes from achievement. Christ is saying that we either do it right or don't do it at all.

At the annunciation when Mary, the Mother of Jesus, was asked by the angel Gabriel to give her word to God, she did it with such integrity that the word she spoke became the 'Word made flesh' who came into our world and dwelt among us. Having given her word, it would appear from sacred scripture that Mary remained silent and wordless for the rest of her life. And she said to Gabriel, 'Behold the handmaid of the Lord.Let it be done on to me according to your Word.'

Prayer of the Faithful

Gathered as God's family, we join with Christians everywhere and open our hearts and minds to the Lord, who calls us to follow him, with loving and generous hearts.

1. For our Holy Father and all who are called to leadership within the church. May they read the sign of the times and be attentive to the needs of the present age.
   Lord, hear us.

2. For married couples and those preparing for matrimony, that the Lord will increase their love for one another. May they live their lives to the full and may their personal commitment grow stronger every day.
   Lord, hear us.

3. For those preparing for the priesthood or called to the religious life. May the Lord grant them generous hearts and keep them faithful to their commitment.
   Lord, hear us

4. For the sick of the parish and those suffering or in any kind of need. May the Lord cross their path, calm their fears and be their comfort and support.
   Lord, hear us

5. For all those who have died. May they share eternal life and find in the Lord's presence, true and everlasting peace.
   Lord, hear us.

Heavenly Father, hear the prayer of your people gathered before you. Grant us the courage to accept whatever cross may come our way and always do what is best in the sight of God. We make our prayer through Christ, our Lord. Amen.

14th Sunday in Ordinary Time
First Reading: Isaiah 66:10-14;
Second Reading: Galatians 6:14-18; Gospel: Luke 10:1-12, 17-29

Excitement is in the air as Luke describes the sending forth of the seventy-two disciples on their first missionary engagement. Here we witness the beginning of the greatest adventure story the world has ever known. The disciples are being commissioned to adopt the lifestyle of the wandering preacher and go out and announce the good news of the gospel. They are to get on with the job of preaching and healing without any distractions or hesitations. 'Carry no purse, no haversack, no sandals', because the task is urgent and the need is great. Jesus warned them that the road ahead would not be easy and among other things, opposition would involve the pain of rejection. 'I am sending you out like lambs among wolves.' Christ is making it clear that single-minded and dedicated followers are needed for the building of his kingdom. Half hearted loyalty would not suffice.

What is most important is that this invitation is extended to the church in every age and in every place. The whole church is missionary and the work of evangelisation is an essential duty of the people of God. This is a reminder that the task of promoting the teaching of Jesus Christ does not belong to a few but is given rightly to us all. No one can escape this most basic responsibility, for if we fail to be involved the church will suffer. In former times the preaching of Christianity was left up to priests and religious. People in the congregation were inclined to leave religious instruction to the experts. There was the general feeling that others were better qualified for the task and to talk about religion was downright embarrassing. However, as followers of Jesus we are called to make known the Christian message wherever we go because it is alive and relevant to every life. In an age of disillusionment people are thirsting for God to fill the vacuum of emptiness in their lives. People are hungry for truth about life. They want to be told things that will give them strength, comfort and a sense of direction. Many who are hurting are eagerly waiting to hear that God is calling them beyond the narrow confines of their present situation and is offering them joy beyond their imagining. In Christ they can find comfort in their sorrow and meaning in their struggle. The Lord relies on us as he relied on his disciples to bring his healing and consolation to those afflicted. We bring the good news to others by the witness of our lives and we do not have to cross our doorstep in order to do it. Parents do this as a matter of course any time they instruct their children in the difference between what is right and what is wrong. So do young people who have the courage to stand their ground and speak out when wrong is being done rather than stay silent and fall in with the prevailing culture. In a world where pain and suffering seem to reign, simple things like a friendly smile, a word of thanks, a gentle touch can work wonders and show that we care. The sending out of the seventy-two symbolises the start of Christ's mission to bring peace and reconciliation to humankind. For some, peace conjures up visions of a calm sea and a blue sky, a place where we can listen to the sounds of nature and observe the beauty of God's creation or the rest that comes at the end of a busy day. For others it means the laying down of weapons and the absence of war. But the gospel speaks of the peace of Christ, a peace that the world cannot give.

The goal of the disciples' mission was peace but preaching it would all be futile if they had not got it themselves. There can be no peace until we find peace with God who wants us to know peace in every area of our lives – peace in our daily work, in our family and in our homes. When the demands of life press in on us and we are weary in body and soul, we can call out to God for his peace. However, we will never know true peace if we are constantly striving for bigger and better things rather than being satisfied with what we have. To enjoy a little happiness we must accept life just as it is now. This means being fulfilled at our work, embracing the people around us, accepting them with their faults and failings, and enjoying contentment in our family relationships.

Prayer of the Faithful

As God's holy people called in different ways to spread the gospel and to bring peace to the world, we turn to the Father who is the Lord of the harvest and make our prayer.

1. For the leaders of the church, that they may develop a deepening sense of mission in their work of gathering together the scattered children of God.
   Lord, hear us.

2. For those who have given their lives to God as foreign missionaries: may they have the support of the community they have left behind and receive a welcome from those to whom they are sent.
   Lord, hear us.

3. We now pray for farmers who till the soil and work the land, that they may have good weather and a plentiful harvest.
   Lord, hear us.

4. For those who minister to the sick and look after the dying, that they may be ever conscious of the dignity of their calling.
   Lord, hear us.

5. Grant peace and eternal rest to the faithful departed especially those for whom we have been asked to pray.
   Lord, hear us.

Gracious and loving God, give us the strength to respond to your invitation of sharing in the mission of your Son in all the aspects of our lives. Help us consecrate ourselves anew to the service of your gospel and to work for the glory of your name. We make our prayer through Christ, our Lord. Amen

15th Sunday in Ordinary Time
First Reading: Deuteronomy 30:10-14;
Second Reading: Colossians 1:15-20; Gospel: Luke 10:25-37

Church attendance may be down but that does not necessarily mean people are not seriously concerned about matters religious. In a recent survey taken in one of the larger cities of England, people were asked: 'If you could meet God and put one question to him, what would it be?' Remarkably the question most people wanted an answer for was, 'Is there an eternal life and how can I get it?' The lawyer in the gospel may have been out to trick Jesus but there was no doubt that he was asking a very good question. Jesus meets the challenge by putting the answer in practical human terms. He tells the famous gospel story about the Good Samaritan, from which 2,000 years later one of our leading help organisations derives it name.

We are all familiar with 'no go' areas in our own cites and towns which are to be avoided at all costs and where it is a danger to walk the streets at night. The road from Jerusalem to Jericho was like that. It was really just a track winding its way downhill for seventeen miles and twisted around huge boulders. Given its location, it was a favourite haunt for robbers and outlaws. Travelling down that road alone was foolhardy and a risky business. Only a fool would set out on such a journey without companions for protection. Half way down that road, the victim in Jesus' story is robbed of his money, beaten within an inch of his life and left for dead in the ditch.

Of the three people who come on the scene only one stops to administer help to the poor wretch. Acting within the strict limits of their religion, the priest and the Levite passed him by, as it would be unbecoming for them to associate with the poor. These two churchy people were on their way to the temple and their religious rules prevented them from coming to the aid of the stricken man. For them religious purity ranked higher than compassion. The shock to the system is that compassion does come and from a most unexpected source, a Samaritan. This outsider who is despised by the Jews as an ignorant and irreligious half-breed, binds the victim's wounds, takes him to safety and foots the bill for his care. He goes beyond the limits of religion to extend the boundary of compassion. When the story is over it is the turn of Jesus to ask the lawyer, 'Which of these three do you think proved himself a neighbour to the man who fell into the brigand's hands?' And he is told to go and do likewise – to go and be a good neighbour.

'Who is my neighbour?' is always an awkward and leading question! While it is easy to profess love for people in general, it is more of a challenge to love individuals specifically. Our neighbour is not necessarily someone who lives in the same street, or the people we are friendly with and who are good company, but anyone who needs our help, like the elderly lady across the street or an aged parent in a nursing home. Caring is a risky business and is very demanding. It takes courage to reach out to someone who is hurting as it involves personal contact, giving of our time, putting ourselves out and the doing of things which are inconvenient. We salve our conscience in this regard by placing a contribution in the Vincent de Paul box or making a donation to some worthwhile charitable cause. Anyway we are too busy with family and work to be really bothered.

This parable, which powerfully demonstrates that all people are worthy of being loved, regardless of race or religion, invites us to examine our relationship with other people and to ask ourselves 'What is our response to people in need? Do we stop and offer help or do we pass by?' All too often we walk the human pathway and miss the victims on the sidewalk. Refugees and homeless people have their own story to tell. We are closer to the priest and the levite than we would care to imagine. Compassion is having a heart that is open to everyone seeking our help. The whole focus of the story is to have eyes to see other people's pain, ears to hear the cry in their voices and to be there when needed to rescue the broken hearted. If we fail in loving our neighbour, how can we succeed in loving God?

Prayer of the Faithful

Humbled and moved by the compassion of God who makes the sun shine and the rain fall on the rich and the poor alike, we come in faith and gratitude to make our petitions.

1. That the members of Christ's church throughout the world may be conscious of the needs of the people around them, especially those who suffer in their midst.
   Lord, hear us.

2. That those in the caring professions, doctors, nurses, ambulance personnel and home helps, may carry out their work with Christ-like compassion and bring comfort and meaning to broken lives.
   Lord, hear us.

3. That those who utter racist, ethnic and sexist remarks and whose hearts are heavily laden down with a burden of bitterness will come to realise that their comments are contrary to the law of God.
   Lord, hear us.

4. Lord, hear our prayer for neighbours who in good times shared our joy and laughter and who in times of trouble and sorrow shared our pain and grief.
   Lord, hear us.

5. For those who have died, especially those who have no one left on earth to pray for them.
   Lord, hear us.

Heavenly Father, accept our prayers and send your Holy Spirit to speak to us in and through the experience of our daily lives. As we struggle on the road to your kingdom, may we see our work as an extension of Christ's love to the world. We make this prayer through Christ, our Lord. Amen

16th Sunday in Ordinary Time

First Reading: Genesis 18:1-10;
Second Reading: Colossians 1:24-28; Gospel: Luke 10:38-42

This gospel story as narrated by Luke is meant to surprise us, make us sit up and start thinking. In almost every age of the church it has succeeded in doing this by provoking light-hearted controversy. The truth is that throughout history Christians have felt aggrieved on behalf of Martha. As long ago as the fourth century, the 'Desert Fathers' commented that it was because Martha worked that Mary could be praised. St Teresa of Avila remarked that if Martha had behaved like Mary, Christ would have gone hungry. Maybe it is because so much emphasis is placed upon achievement and the fact that we define ourselves by our busyness, assuming that the more we do the more worthwhile we will appear to be. After all, the heroes in every age are those who make money, carve out successful careers, become famous and build personal empires. We have a lot of sympathy for Martha and can understand the frustration that led to her impatient outburst because we like to keep ourselves occupied and hate wasting time.

At the outset we have got to remember Martha and Mary were both good people and along with their brother Lazarus were close friends of Christ. Their home on the outskirts of Jerusalem was an oasis of peace and a place where he was welcome and could feel very much at ease. For Christ to make a remark that would be dismissive of Martha or disparaging of her work would be completely out of character. Perhaps Jesus knew that he was on his way to Jerusalem for the last time and contemplating what lay ahead was so worrisome that he needed to talk and to share his anxiety with friends. This being the case, he would not have come specifically for a meal but to be among friends. While Martha fussed around preparing a meal, Mary sensed what Jesus really wanted and responded to his need by sitting at his feet and silently listening.

We all know people who are like the two sisters. There is the 'hands on' person who like Martha can see to it that a job is done efficiently and right now. Then there is Mary the dreamer who is less inclined to be in a hurry and has all the time in the world to sit at ease and listen to a troubled soul. While we can measure the amount of work a Martha makes to the smooth running of life it is not so easy to quantify the contribution a Mary presents. There are shades of the Martha and Mary in our makeup. They are the two sides of our personality that need to be in harmony if we are to live a proper Christian life. Balancing the two – the contemplative and the active – to the best of our ability is the challenge we all have to face because in our harried and noisy world, the Martha is inclined to smother the Mary. Busyness can so easily take over and dominate our lives. We are always preoccupied with the amount of work that is to be done and distracted by so much activity that there is precious little time for reflection. We end up neglecting prayer, which helps us keep everything in proper perspective. Excessive ongoing activity can burn us up and block out any sense of the spiritual. We can get so involved in day to day living that we forget the overall purpose of life and the fact that there is more to our lives than the work we perform.

This gospel invites us to step back from the hustle and bustle of life and reflect on how to show proper hospitality to people in need. We read how Abraham's enthusiastic and extravagant display of hospitality to the three strangers at the oak of Mamre is rewarded by the generosity of God. His wife Sarah who is now in her old age and has been barren will bear a child. We can risk hospitality because God does not forget us. The story of God coming among his people in the guise of a stranger appears in many religious traditions. It is captured in the old Irish runic verse:

I saw a stranger yesterday,
I put food for him in the eating-place,
drink for him in the drinking place,
and music for him in the listening place,
and he blessed me and my people.
and later I heard the lark singing,
'tis often, often, often,
that Christ comes in the guise of a stranger.

We can never be sure under what likeness God will come and pay us a visit. The heart of hospitality is attention to a stranger.

Prayer of the Faithful

Gathered together as God's family and confident of his mercy and compassion we place before the Father our petitions and needs.

1. We pray for the church throughout the world. May she welcome graciously all passers-by who come seeking comfort, guidance and help.
   Lord, hear us.

2. Grant us the grace to become an open and welcoming community towards God's needy children who feel abandoned, left out in the cold or rejected.
   Lord, hear us.

3. We pray for ourselves, that like Mary we may choose the better part and invite Jesus into our hearts and homes as an honoured guest.
   Lord, hear us.

4. We bring before you, the worried, the anxious, the lonely, the sick and the bereaved. May they experience the peace of your presence.
   Lord, hear us.

5. We pray for the faithful departed whose journey of faith is over: may they enjoy the full revelation of Christ in all his glory at the banquet of eternal life.
   Lord, hear us.

Loving God and Father, you sent your Son among us to seek out and to save the lost. Welcome back into your family all those who have strayed and offer them a place at the banquet of your kingdom. We make our prayer through Christ, our Lord. Amen.

17th Sunday in Ordinary Time
First Reading: Genesis 18:20-32;
Second Reading: Colossians 2:12-14; Gospel: Luke 11:1-13

There is a story told of two sisters who hadn't spoken for years. One took seriously ill, so the other sister felt obliged to visit her in hospital. They seemed to have got on well, made things up and to have found forgiveness. But when the sister was leaving the sick room, the other said: 'And by the way, if I get better, we go back to the way we were.' When we find ourselves reeling off the familiar words of the 'Our Father' at Mass, I wonder how many of us realise that its plea for forgiveness is based on our willingness to forgive those who have offended us? The 'Our Father' is more than a collection of words to be memorised. It is a prayer to be lived if we are willing to change and turn our lives completely towards God.

There is a vast difference between praying and saying prayers. As children growing up, most of us were taught many prayers but few of us were actually taught how to pray. It is an art form where most of us are ill at ease. We try to pray but we are so hopeless at it that we are inclined to turn to prayer as a last resort. The disciples were obviously experiencing some difficulty with their prayer life when on their way to Jerusalem for the last time they asked Jesus to teach them how to pray. They had often seen him withdraw from their company to be at prayer and realised that it was from this heart to heart conversation with God that he drew the strength and spiritual energy that sustained him in his preaching. It did not come as a surprise that when Jesus responded to their request on how to pray he had no hesitation in telling them to address God as Father. The image of God as a parent is meant to inspire confidence in us. Not only that, but we are to approach him with the trust of children who know that they are loved.

One of the better definitions of prayer is to describe it as a heart to heart conversation with a friend. Friendship is something we all appreciate as an essential human experience and few things in life are more precious. Our relationship with God is not so very different from our relationships with our best friends. Prayer links us to God in friendship and, on our part, it is a reaching out to grasp Our Father's outstretched, welcoming hand. The purpose of prayer is to deepen our relationship with God and like all relationships it must be worked at and constantly renewed. It also helps us to peel away all our pretensions and discover in all honesty who we really are. Thomas Merton put it well in his book 'Seeds of Contemplation' when he said: 'If I find God, I find myself, and if I find my true self I will find God.'

The 'Our Father' teaches us as much about prayer as we need to know. It is a simple prayer that begins by praising God with a wish that life in our community and in our world might reflect more of his presence and be lived with respectful reverence according to his values. We pray for our daily needs like nourishment for our bodies, healing for our relationships and forgiveness for our wrong doings. Part of the problem that we have with prayer comes from focusing on our wants instead of our needs. In daily life we need so little but our consumer society encourages us to want so much. Asking the Lord in prayer is not a matter of drawing up a list of wants for our own personal gratification but an entrusting of our lives into his hands for safe keeping. More often than not, the Lord doesn't seem to be in a hurry to answer our request. That is why praying for someone whom we know is facing a crisis in their life is less a matter of asking for an immediate remedy for their insurmountable problem as the bringing of a fresh understanding to help them cope with their pain.

When we pray the Lord's Prayer at this eucharistic banquet we come here from different walks of life and assemble as a community of sinners painfully aware that before God we have all fallen short and are greatly in need of his mercy. The church is a refuge for sinners and not a sanctuary for saints.

Prayer of the Faithful

With unlimited confidence in God and in his love we present our needs and requests as brothers and sisters with a common Father.

1. For all who exercise ministry in the church and are charged with shepherding the flock of Christ: may the Lord grant them a deep trust and strength in the office they hold.
   Lord, hear us.

2. For those who have lost faith in prayer and trust in God: may they be inspired by the confidence of Abraham and find new joy in God's loving kindness.
   Lord, hear us.

3. For those who are on vacation and resting from strenuous work: may they find this time of peaceful relaxation an opportunity for spiritual growth.
   Lord, hear us.

4. For all who are ill and for those in special care: may they find happiness through the kindness and support of all of us.
   Lord, hear us.

5. For the faithful departed: may they see the Lord face to face and come to rejoice in his presence forever.
   Lord, hear us.

God of glory and majesty, teach us to confidently ask, to joyfully seek, to hopefully knock and when life is difficult never to grow weary of trusting in your loving ways. Help us to accept your will, through Christ, our Lord. Amen

18th Sunday in Ordinary Time

First Reading: Genesis 18:20-32;
Second Reading: Colossians 2:12-14; Gospel: Luke 11:1-13

The ancient Greeks had a saying, 'Greed is like drinking sea water – the more you drink the thirstier you become', and how apt that comment is in relation to this gospel reading. A man in the crowd who wanted Christ to take his side in a dispute with his brother over a matter of family inheritance is told very bluntly to avoid greed in all its forms. He provides Jesus with an opportunity to tell the story of the foolish farmer, blessed with a bumper harvest, whose reaction is not to be content with his good fortune but to build bigger and better barns. What he wants is absolute security for the future. His world is seen in terms of what he owns and is unrelated to the fortune or fate of any other human being. Nothing else matters. He has lost the run of himself, becomes immortal in his own eyes and has forgotten that life is not made secure by possessions. Before he has a chance to relax and enjoy his wealth he has no life left. He is called back home to his maker. He had forgotten that life on earth was God's to give and God's to take away.

Ever since Cain killed his brother Abel, greed and envy have been the root cause of a great deal of our unhappiness. So many of our problems, our unnecessary worries and our sleepless nights are over possessions. In every generation people have murdered, wars have raged and families have been torn apart by the unbridled desire to have more than our neighbour. We all know about family rifts, of squabbles over wills, with not a thought given to deceased relatives. What's more, the poor can be as greedy as the rich, for deep down in all of us is the streak of avarice, the hoarding instinct, the craving to want more and never be satisfied.

Jesus uses the man's death in the story to put wealth and prosperity into their proper perspective by giving us the stark reminder that we are not completely in control of our lives. As the old Irish saying goes: 'There are no pockets in a shroud.' We cannot bring our wealth with us. The hearse does not stop at the bank and money cannot purchase peace of mind not to speak of it buying our way into heaven. Riches, as Jesus often points out are a danger to the soul. Nevertheless, the fact that we cannot bring our wealth with us when we die, does not prevent us being competitive and ambitious and having a sneaking regard for the man who has made it. Our over materialistic culture is convinced that bigger is better and equates who we are with what we acquire. There are things which possess us, and having more often results in enjoying less with each new success, creating an added thirst. We are so intent in heaping up riches, being attached to the latest gadget and in storing up short-term wealth that we forget what the future is really about. Maybe it is time to curtail our wants for, while the goods of the earth are essential to enhance life, they do not satisfy the deepest longings of the human heart.

While the acquisition of wealth is not being outrightly condemned, Jesus is knocking the foolish idea of placing undue emphasis on material riches at the expense of spiritual treasures. The readings challenge us to think about fundamental issues like what is the meaning of life? Where do I find fulfilment? What are my hopes and dreams for tomorrow? Have I ever thought about the hereafter? When I die, what will count is the person I have become in the course of living and not the wealth I have acquired along the way. We need reminding that there is more to us than our material comforts. Being rich in the sight of God who is the source of all good brings into sharp focus the real purpose of life.

Let's not forget that life is short and passes by very quickly. It has no second act or repeat performance and it is all too easy to become entangled in the things that are passing away. That is why it is important to make good use of time God gives us. Wouldn't it be great at the end of life to look back on our days on earth and be able to say: I lived by Christian values; I was a good parent who reared the family as best I could. I got on well with the neighbours and offered help where it was needed in the local community. I always valued people not for what they earn or their social standing but for who they are in the sight of God.

Prayer of the Faithful

With renewed confidence we turn to the Father, the source of all good things, who, out of the generosity of his heart, has shown us the way to his kingdom by sending his Son Jesus as our guide.

1. We pray for the church: may she proclaim justice and integrity in the world and be the living embodiment of God's concern for those in distress.
   Lord, hear us.

2. For our political leaders, that they may work untiringly to ensure a fair distribution of the wealth of the country.
   Lord, hear us.

3. Help us to get our personal priorities in tune with gospel values so that we may realise that the most precious things in life – health, friendship, inward peace and goodness of heart – are things that money can not purchase.
   Lord, hear us.

4. May God grant restored health to the sick and may they find support in their faith and in the care and prayer of their friends.
   Lord, hear us.

5. For those who have died recently and who have gone before us, that they may enjoy the glory of the Risen Christ.
   Lord, hear us.

Lord God, you are the rock on which we stand, listen to our prayer. Teach us true Christian detachment from earthly possessions and inspire us with an awareness of the passing nature of the world so that we may live with our heart set on the things of heaven. We make our prayer through Christ, our Lord. Amen

19th Sunday in Ordinary Time
First Reading: Wisdom 18:6-9;
Second Reading: Hebrews 11:1-2, 8-19; Gospel: Luke 12:32-48

The pages of the bible are filled with stories of people who had outstanding faith – people who believed what God promised and acted on those beliefs at a cost to themselves. In spite of great suffering, loneliness and isolation these mighty heroes of the past remained faithful. The lives of ancestral figures like Abraham and spiritual giants like Moses are so morally and spiritually uplifting that their exploits were recalled at times when the Jewish people's morale was low or when they felt their cultural identity endangered. Remembering the lives of these dynamic characters, shrouded in the mists of time, was instrumental in giving encouragement to those who were faltering in faith and weak in their resolve. The inspiration Israelites drew from listening to stories, which recalled past glories, acted as a spiritual tonic and gave them the courage to live meaningfully and with purpose in their present situation.

The first reading, from the Book of Wisdom, recalls the Exodus, that never to be forgotten drama in the life of Israel when Moses, indifferent to the king's blind rage, turned his heel on Egypt and went forth with the Hebrew people through the Red Sea which parted to give them dry ground and let them escape to safety. After centuries of suffering, Moses led his people out of slavery and across the wilderness to the Promised Land. The decision to flee the land of their oppressor at the very time the angel of death was visiting the first born of every Egyptian household, was openly defiant but it was a risk taken on the strength of their leader's faith in God's call to free his people. Somehow Moses left his mark on his people in a way that was never to be forgotten. His name conveyed powerful images of holiness, leadership and self-confidence. He was the central actor in the great drama of the Exodus and gave his people the constant reassurance that long after he had gone God would still look after them. I don't know how Moses would have fared in an opinion poll. He was not a popular leader and when the going got tough, there were lots of rebellions against him.

However, he was a man of faith and his influence has lasted longer than anyone else in human history. I find it moving that the Pharaohs, who held absolute power in the world of their day, are no more while the Israelites whom they once enslaved still live. Moses arrived at the border of the Promised Land but never actually entered its territory. He died not having achieved what was promised. Nevertheless that did not prevent him from answering God's call to lead his people to freedom.

It's a long way from Moses and Exodus to our present age. Although Moses is a distant figure he lives on in the many men and women who endure the hardship that comes their way and still go forward in faith. When you come to think about it, Exodus means no more than a way out, a way out from bondage. There is bondage and brokenness of spirit in our age, which is just as real as what the Israelites suffered in Egypt under the Pharaohs. We may be living in a thoroughly modern society but brokenness of spirit is everywhere. We see it in the deserted wife whose world is shattered and whose children are fatherless. It's all around us in lives threatened by drug addiction, by fear of abandonment in old age and by those condemned to despair and poverty. The Israelites looked back to Moses as the man who gave them encouragement in times of difficulty. He put his trust in God, kept looking ahead and with eyes fixed on the Promised Land he never stopped going forward.

As a pilgrim people who are often blinded by worry and overburdened with insecurity, we are called like Moses to make that leap of faith and place our trust in God who leads us by ways and means that defy understanding. It is through faith that we cling to the essence of our dreams when they seem to be dashed before our eyes. Faith is our answer to God's call and is evident in the pattern of our behaviour and in the way we live. Above all it is a willingness to put our life on the line for God.

Prayer of the Faithful

Gathered together as descendants of Abraham, in a spirit of trusting reverence, we make our prayer to the Father who is the support of the weak and the protector of the needy.

1. We pray that the leaders of the church will live up to the trust given them by exercising stewardship of the Lord's household wisely.
   Lord, hear us.

2. For those holding public office, that they will seek not their own interests but the good of the people whom they govern.
   Lord, hear us.

3. For those who have lost a sense of direction in their lives and are disillusioned with religion, alienated from the church and adrift on the sea of life. May they find a path that will lead them towards the light.
   Lord, hear us.

4. For the sick, the poor, the lonely and the oppressed: may the Lord of all support and comfort them.
   Lord, hear us.

5. For the faithful departed, that they experience the fullness of the Lord's merciful presence.
   Lord, hear us.

Heavenly Father, sustain us on our pilgrim way. Keep us true to the faith you have given us and help us to live our lives so that, one day, we may enjoy eternal happiness in heaven. We make our prayer through Christ, our Lord. Amen.

20th Sunday in Ordinary Time
First Reading: Jeremiah 38:4-6, 8-10;
Second Reading: Hebrews 12:1-4; Gospel: Luke 12:49-53

The lonely and tragic figure of Jeremiah gives us an unusual insight into the people charged with bringing God's message to the Jewish nation. He lived in a troubled time due to wars and power struggles in the Middle East. His vocation as a prophet for almost forty years brought enormous sacrifices because of the truth that he spoke. Time and time again his voice rang out across the land as he confronted both rulers and people who had broken the Covenant and put their trust in the false Gods of military alliances. He reminded those who had become arrogant in their exercise of power that they were answerable to God. What kept him going and made his pain worthwhile was the firm belief that, no matter what happened or how much he suffered, God was with him.

The small kingdom of Judah was caught in a pincer movement between two mighty powers, Egypt to the south and Babylon to the north. Jeremiah prophesied that Jerusalem would fall at the hands of the Babylonians and counselled surrender so that citizens' lives would be spared and the destruction of the city averted. It was an unpopular message and was regarded as an act of treason by the authorities. They accused him of sedition and demanded the prophet's death for undermining military morale, having a defeatist attitude and weakening the will of the people to resist. Speaking the truth to those in power is never easy and Jeremiah paid the price. He was arrested, thrown into a muddy cistern where he was left to drown but was eventually saved by the intervention of a kindly foreigner.

Wherever he went, Jeremiah was all the time challenging the establishment. In his life there was no room for compromise. He had a mission to fulfil with painful consequences and he pulled no punches. Jeremiah refused to butter up the king by telling him what he and the people wanted to hear. Life would have been a lot easier for him if he had gone along with the flow and not made a fuss. History remembers Jeremiah as a disturbing figure who shaped an identity for the Jewish people. He was smuggled out of Jerusalem during the sacking of the city and ended his days in Egypt.

In any age the role of the prophet is not an easy one. Suffering for one's belief is not something confined to the past. There are everyday examples closer to home of people who have found themselves marginalised and labelled troublemakers for sticking to their principles. Standing for something inevitably means standing against a lot of other things. God's word, which highlights injustice, falsehood and oppression in a society, is not always welcome, and neither are God's messengers. In every age, shooting the messenger for bringing bad news is a long-standing human tradition. When things go wrong, it is important to find a scapegoat and shift the blame. In some parts of the world it is dangerous to be a Christian and many have given their lives because their faith led them to speak out against corruption, cruelty and violence.

The chances of being called to put our life on the line for our faith are remote; but the persecution may be more subtle. While the gospel message challenges us to stand up and be counted, most of us would prefer to keep our faith a private matter. There is always the fear that if it were known around the work place that we attend church, are faithful to our wedded spouse, that we pray and live by the commandments, we may be laughed at and labelled old fashioned. Likewise, young persons who say no to the drug culture and to lives fuelled by alcohol will find themselves facing animosity and ridicule for being out of step with their peers. Loyalty to Jesus is challenging because it demands rowing upstream against the flow of public opinion. Discipleship involves taking a stand on certain issues and making choices that will bring tension and conflict with the life around us. We would prefer if our religion was comfortable and had a feel good factor that made people happy. Jesus knew that the Christian message when preached or lived with conviction would arouse anger and cause division because it would expose corruption and highlight injustice. Do we dare speak words of truth and stand up for the principles laid down by the teachings of Jesus Christ? For evil to triumph, all that is necessary is for good people to remain silent.

Prayer of the Faithful

Full of confidence we approach the Father who protects us with his powerful love and is a light and a support to all who are in need.

1. We pray that the leaders of the church may have the insight and wisdom to interpret our times and the courage to speak the word of God without fear in every season and place.
   Lord, hear us.

2. For those who are feeling the pain of discipleship and are suffering for their principles: may they remain constant in their faith and may the strength of God be with them in their trials.
   Lord, hear us.

3. For families who are divided and whose lives have become embittered with conflict: may they know the grace of forgiveness and find ways of resolving their differences.
   Lord, hear us.

4. For the sick, the lonely, the downhearted and those who feel they have no purpose in life: that God may sustain them with his Spirit.
   Lord, hear us.

5. We pray for the dead, that they will see God face to face and know him as he really is.
   Lord, hear us.

Heavenly Father, be with us in our time of trial and doubt. Open our hearts to hear the cry of the poor and to respond with courage and generosity. Keep us true to the faith given us through Christ, our Lord. Amen.

21st Sunday in Ordinary Time
First Reading: Isaiah 66:18-21;
Second Reading: Hebrews 12:5-7, 11-13; Gospel: Luke 13:22-30

According to St Paul, the joys of this world are as nothing in comparison to what God has in store for those who love him. We have all wondered from time to time, what heaven will be like and why looking on the face of God will fill us with perfect happiness. We have no direct window on eternal life and the notion of living forever boggles the mind. Our hungry hearts want something that no mere human being can ever give – permanent and perfect happiness, eternal bliss that will never go away. Over the centuries preachers, writers and artists have attempted to describe and explain heaven. They have pictured future existence as one in which there will be no more sorrow or pain and where every tear will be wiped away from our eyes – where there will be an end to mourning and death.

Difficulties arise, however, when we start to wonder who will make it into heaven. We derive comfort from Isaiah who paints a picture of God's unbounded saving grace, which reaches out to people of all nationalities and especially to those on the margins and those who are despised. It portrays the generosity of God in throwing open the kingdom of God to everyone on an equal footing. Heaven is open to all and there are no conditions of entry that will exclude particular groups of individuals. Admission has nothing to do with who you are, whom you know, where you come from or even how perfectly you have abided by the rules. At God's banquet there is no quota system or restriction of numbers. Favouritism has no place in his plan and no special group can claim a privileged position.

However, when Jesus was queried by a passer-by who was keen to know the exact number of people going to be saved, he side-stepped the question but cautioned the bystander against making light of entry into his kingdom. Following him would not be easy and admission should not be taken for granted. He made the point that the gateway to eternal life was a narrow one and there was no gain without pain on the homeward journey. His words were tinged with anger at his fellow countrymen who thought heaven could be won without making an effort. The Jews of his time made the fatal mistake of banking too heavily on their role as God's chosen people and failed to take the offer of salvation seriously. Jesus told them that they relied too much on their relationship with Abraham and accepted too readily the notion that somehow they were an elite group, on the inner track with God.

It would be wrong to give the impression that as Christians we have been issued with free passes into heaven. There is no such thing as cheap grace and we cannot live on the glories of our past Christian history. The Lord is not at all impressed with superficial acquaintances, like having gone on a pilgrimage to The Holy Land, having an uncle in religion, having been to church for a wedding, or attendance at a family christening. We really can't say that because we were baptised under the 'church roof', we are home safe. It is true that we can live next door to someone and have nothing in common. We can listen to what is being said and pay no heed to it. The same can be said of the message of Jesus. We really cannot count ourselves among the friends of Jesus unless we have a life lived in his name. When the moment of reckoning arrives, the self-illusion of prestige and rank are of no advantage, for the cutting edge is whether we will be recognised as genuine disciples. The challenge that the gospel lays before us is to deepen our commitment to Christ and to follow in his footsteps as best we can, in the situations of life that we find ourselves in. We must not isolate Sunday worship from our weekday lives or confine religion to the church. Every day presents us with opportunities to follow Jesus. We proclaim the God we serve in the way we transact our weekday business in our offices, supermarkets and classrooms. The way we live announces to the world that salvation is for all people. God has opened the door but it is up to us to enter. A claim to association with Jesus is not enough. Repentance is called for, otherwise one may find the door locked. Entrance into the kingdom is a question of struggling rather than strolling in.

Prayer of the Faithful

Aware of the challenge to live our lives in conformity with gospel values so as to help make Jesus Christ known to the world, we speak our needs to our heavenly Father who brings us lasting joy in these changing times.

1. That the church will continue to touch the hearts and enlighten the minds of its followers with its vision of peace and justice.
   Lord, hear us.

2. For those who have difficult decisions to make: may they be supported by the love of God, enlightened by the words of his Son and given courage by the Holy Spirit.
   Lord, hear us.

3. Grant to parents the courage and patience to reflect on the meaning of their faith so that they may hand it on to their children as a motivating force to influence their lives.
   Lord, hear us.

4. That the Lord will reveal his love and concern for the sick and for all in any distress of mind or body.
   Lord, hear us.

5. For our departed relatives and friends and for all who have died: may they have light, happiness and peace in the kingdom of God.
   Lord, hear us.

Merciful Father, accept the prayers and sufferings of your people. Give us the grace to rise above our human weaknesses, so that we may be true to your word in all that we say and do through Christ, our Lord. Amen.

22nd Sunday in Ordinary Time
First Reading: Sirach 3:17-20, 28-29;
Second Reading: Hebrews 12:18-19, 22-24; Gospel: Luke 14: 1, 7-14

Meal protocol in the ancient world could be an explosive issue and in the case of some Jewish groups, a religious one also. The seat one occupied at a banquet table was no light matter since it indicated how important was one's standing in the eyes of the host. It was the custom for the more distinguished guests to purposely arrive late so as to make a grand entrance and focus attention on being ushered up into the places of honour. Jesus was no stranger to such gatherings and was comfortable breaking bread with all classes of people. He regarded the meal as the greatest symbol of what life was like with God. Celebrating the Sabbath at the house of a well-known Pharisee where several of the guests jostle in an undignified manner for positions of prestige and power becomes the occasion for teaching a powerful lesson on the importance of humility in our everyday lives.

Living in a world that encourages self-promotion and self-praise, it comes as no surprise that humility is not too well understood. Qualities of gentleness, meekness and courtesy are not in high demand in a society that scrambles for success, self-sufficiency and independence no matter what the cost. On all sides the emphasis is on the reverse. The major obstacle to humility is pride, which lures us into living independently of God and believing that we do not need his help to live our lives. Most of us realise that we are naturally self-centred, full of selfish ambition, always putting ourselves first, wanting the best of everything. We often respond to those around us in ways that make us appear proud, haughty and arrogant. At the same time, few things annoy us more than close neighbours who regard themselves as better than we are. Among all the faults we observe in others, pride is the failing we find most offensive. That is why we love to see the proud person's bubble burst. What is worse: self-seeking puts up an insurmountable barrier between the soul and God. It deceives us into thinking that what we have is truly ours with no thanks due to anyone else. Pride is a road going nowhere but is so endemic in our nature that it goes undetected by all who display it. Like a frost that nips our spiritual growth it makes us self-centred and full of our own importance. It always deceives its owner and cuts us off from reality by making us prisoners of ourselves. In God's eyes the proud man takes a very lowly place and will be excluded from the guest list to the master's banquet.

Humility calls upon us to turn our lives over to God and recognise that all we are and all we do derives ultimately from him. We all have a rough idea of what humility is. It is not pride but neither is it pretence or self-depreciation. In the not too distant past humility was regarded as belittling oneself: like having an inferiority complex. The fact that we were not encouraged to argue our case, defend our corner, complain or speak out in the face of unfairness created a dreadful handicap in our personal dealings with the world. It meant that we were almost apologising for our existence. Humility is no hangdog approach to life. It does not need to pretend anything as it is simply seeing ourselves as we actually are, not higher or lower. It means being up front and gut-level honest about ourselves. St Teresa of Avila says 'humility is the truth about myself and the truth is that I am fearfully and wonderfully made'. 'I am God's work of art' (Eph 2:10), a unique creation. 'I am made a little less than the angels' (Ps 8:5). 'I am loved with an everlasting love' (Jer 31:3). It is no virtue to deny that we have talents or refuse to use them. There is nothing wrong with recognising our virtues and good deeds and thanking God for them. At the same time we must be willing to admit our frailty and take responsibility for our faults and failings, our weakness and waywardness. What makes humility so desirable is the marvellous thing that it does to us, for it creates in us a capacity for the closest possible intimacy with God. It enables us to be at home with mystery, helping us to marvel at the beauty of the world. It beckons us to give due care and attention to the spiritual side of our lives.

Prayer of the Faithful

Conscious of our weakness and our pride we come before the Lord of history in all humility with our needs and petitions.

1. We pray that all those called to exercise leadership in the church may devote themselves generously to serving the poor under their care by acting justly, loving tenderly and walking humbly in the footsteps of Jesus.
   Lord, hear us.

2. Help us to break through our preoccupation with ourselves and to discover the goodness in those around us. May we be sensitive to their feelings and able to put their interests before our own.
   Lord, hear us.

3. We thank you Lord for the life given us: may we never take it for granted but see it as a daily gift from your loving hands.
   Lord, hear us.

4. May we be gentle and caring in reaching out to those in our midst who are poor, sick or troubled in any way.
   Lord, hear us.

5. We remember our beloved dead and pray that they may enter into God's reign of wholeness and peace.
   Lord, hear us.

Lord God, our lives are nothing without you. Help us to realise that it is in giving that we receive and in dying to ourselves that we are born to eternal life. We make this prayer through Christ, our Lord. Amen.

23rd Sunday in Ordinary Time
First Reading: Wisdom 9:13-18;
Second Reading: Philemon 9-10, 12-17; Gospel: Luke 14: 25-33

Have you ever wondered what it would have been like to live in the Palestine of 2000 years ago and to have met the earthly Jesus? On hearing him preach, would you have become one of his followers and headed to Jerusalem with him? Or would you have been like the apostles, who fled when the great moment of crisis arrived! Jesus was on his final journey to the Holy City when he addressed these uncompromising words concerning discipleship to the crowd pressing around and expecting something surprising to happen. They were hoping for the day when as Messiah, he would fulfil their fondest dreams and bring triumph, peace and prosperity to Israel. Jesus knew how unreal these expectations were. These people had no idea of the price they would have to pay as his followers and he was anxious that they recognise what exactly was involved. He was telling them that following him was a serious business. It was not going to be as easy as they thought and it was a decision that could not be taken on impulse or without careful consideration. He cautioned against rushing into discipleship without examining the cost involved. He was at pains to point out that they should not embrace a life of such inevitable sacrifice without the will to see it through to completion. Discipleship was not a pastime but an exacting way of life.

This is a gospel that does not make for comfortable reading. The parables that it contains are a call to take stock and become aware of what is going on in the world. We live in a society where great emphasis is placed upon prestige, power and material possessions. What is more, we define ourselves by what we own and have come to believe that we are what we possess. A glance at a daily paper or glossy magazine is proof that we are a permissive culture that worships the false gods of sex, alcohol, drugs and corporate greed. In our moral confusion we revere youth, cultivate celebrity, honour intelligence and hanker after designer labels. The problem is: how can we pay attention to the things of God if we are part of a culture so preoccupied with the idols of our own choosing? Even our religious worship has lost its bite and has become comfortable. In our own easy-going way we all like to think that we are followers of Christ. We say our prayers in a routine manner, go to Mass on Sundays and do our best to live Christian lives. Yet, when gospel values clash with our way of thinking we have no difficulty in compromising and we pick and choose from Christ's teaching what suits ourselves.

This is a gospel call to change our mindset and to turn our backs on much that the modern world loves and regards as precious. It will not come easy and will even invite ridicule and may mean the parting of the ways with former associates. Strange at it may seem, it is not so much the goods of this world, which prevent us from following Jesus more closely as our attitude to them. The difficulty arises when we spend all our time and energy securing possessions or acquiring more, as if nothing else matters, especially the state of our soul. It is then we become possessed by the things we own, as well as by greed and covetousness. Renouncing possessions doesn't necessarily mean giving them away but developing a spirit of detachment, which prevents them from becoming our whole life's concern. It is all a matter of where our hearts are. We could do worse than spend a few moments in reflection as to what comes first in our lives. What are the things that light up our lives, that give us meaning and keep us going from moment to moment? Would we feel the pinch if we were separated from them? Social conventions must give way to the demands of the Lord. The words of Jesus bring us face to face with the cost of discipleship and the relative importance of all human commitments when compared with our following of Jesus. While discipleship may be demanding it is not impossible. To put Jesus centre stage in our lives will involve sacrifice and the cross. It may mean taking time out to visit a neighbour who is old and infirm but this will make us a more loving person. There is a story told of a man who died and met Jesus who said to him: 'Show me your wounds.' 'But Lord, I have no wounds,' was the man's reply. Jesus looked at him and asked, 'Was there nothing in life worth fighting for?' Carrying the cross is part of being a disciple.

Prayer of the Faithful

Conscious of our weakness but aware that our struggle to live according to the ideals of Jesus is worthwhile, we call upon God for the gift of the Spirit to empower us.

1. For church leaders that they may be inspired to preach the message of Christ in an attractive and authentic manner.
   Lord, hear us.

2. For those who suffer with the cross weighing heavily on their shoulders because of their living of the gospel message: may they hold fast and may Christ sustain them with his grace and hope.
   Lord, hear us.

3. That amid the uncertainties of a changing world we may keep our eyes fixed on Christ and follow him with an unwavering commitment.
   Lord, hear us.

4. For the poor, the sick and those with special needs, that, as a believing community, we may support them in their suffering and need.
   Lord, hear us.

5. We pray for all those who died recently and for all whose anniversaries occur around this time, that they may rise to the fullness of life.
   Lord, hear us.

Heavenly Father, help us to have the power of the gospel at work within our lives so that we may see Christ more clearly and love him more dearly, day by day. Amen.

24th Sunday in Ordinary Time

First Reading: Exodus 32:7-11, 13-14;
Second Reading: 1 Tim 1:12-17; Gospel: Luke 15:1-32

Of all the tragedies that beset ordinary domestic life, none can compare with the pain caused by a family member going missing. It is every parent's worst nightmare. When the missing person fails to return home, neighbours are alerted, the alarm is raised, the police are informed and a widespread search is launched. We have all listened to heartfelt appeals on radio and seen photographs of missing persons posted in public places as well as flashed up on TV screens. There are websites dedicated to the search for missing persons. Families, at their wits end with worry, try everything in an effort to make contact but are rarely successful. The harsh reality is that hundreds of people disappear every year and most of them are never heard of again. Family members die and go to their graves without ever knowing of their whereabouts. We have only got to think of a mother in such a circumstance. While time may have made the disappearance little more than a statistic in the neighbourhood, not a day passes without her thinking of her lost offspring. Every time the doorbell sounds, the telephone rings or a letter drops in the hallway she thinks that it is news of her loved one. At night-time a window may be left slightly open with a bed prepared in the hope that the endless waiting will be soon be over. A mother never gives up the search and clings on to every glimmer of hope no matter how slight. Sleepless nights are spent agonising over her lost-one being somewhere, crying out for help and she is powerless and unable to be of assistance. The pain of endless waiting and wondering becomes unbearable. The mother's life goes on hold.

This morning's gospel, which is a collection of three parables about the Lost Sheep, the Lost Coin and the Lost Son, provides us with material for reflection. The emphasis is on a gracious God who is so much in love with us that he seeks out the lost and forgotten. We are always somewhat anxious and at a loss. Lostness in one form or another is a state of mind and an uneasy feeling that we all share. Parents feel at a loss, unsure of what to do while bringing up a family in a world that is so different to that of their own childhood. There is the lostness of young people who are part of a youth culture that promises so much happiness and excitement but fails to deliver on its dream. There is the lostness of senior citizens sidelined in a society that no longer sees value in old age. There is the lostness of the poor who don't count and are on the margins in a wealthy global economy. There is the personal anxiety that we may have slipped off God's radar screen and have been lost. Many of us today have gone astray and are more morally lost and spiritually confused than we care to realise. That happens as a result of living aimless lives, doing our own thing and indulging in varying forms of escapism.

One commentator on the Lost Coin tells us that the woman in the parable represents each of us searching for our lost humanity. The lost coin represents our heart and soul, which can only be discovered within our very own person by shining the light of Christ into our deepest depths. What is emphasised in the Lost Sheep is the intensity of joy in the heart of God at the return of a single soul that has been separated from him. Time spent searching is not wasted but very much worthwhile. Each of us is important and each of us counts. The Lord's wish is that every sinner should be saved for in his home there is room for all. The final lost and found story about the Prodigal Son contains a compelling message of forgiveness that goes to the hearts of parents who know only too well this heart-wrenching experience in their own lives. The problem of wayward children and heart-broken parents hasn't changed much down the centuries. Everything is greener out there on the other side of the fence and the good life in enjoyable until things start to fall apart; then emptiness, disillusionment and frustration set in. God lets us make our mistakes and learn our lessons but in his mercy, compassion and forgiveness is always scanning the horizon watching and awaiting our return to the fold. It is a wonderful and amazing thought that the Lord loves and cherishes each individual soul in such a personal manner.

Prayer of the Faithful

In humility we now petition our heavenly Father who is rich in mercy to all who call upon him. We ask for an increase in faith so that we can bring his peace and forgiveness to our brothers and sisters.

1. We pray for the leaders of the church that they may faithfully watch over the flock of Christ, seeking out the lost, healing the wounded and bringing the good news of God's welcoming forgiveness to all humanity.
   Lord, hear us.

2. For all who have abandoned the Father's house, that the love and faith of the Christian community may help them find their way home.
   Lord, hear us.

3. For families who are estranged and torn apart by misunderstandings and hurts, that God's healing power may bring them together in love.
   Lord, hear us.

4. For the sick, for those who struggle with depression and despair, that they may be touched by the healing power of God's mercy and compassion.
   Lord, hear us.

5. For our relatives and friends who have died and all for whom we have been asked to pray: may God reward their faithfulness in the everlasting feast of heaven.
   Lord, hear us.

Loving and forgiving God, who welcomes home the sinner and extends his saving love to all, guide us in your gentle mercy, help us to rid ourselves of our pride and anger and teach us to forgive all who harm us. We make our prayer through Christ, our Lord. Amen.

25th Sunday in Ordinary Time
First Reading: Amos 8:4-7;
Second Reading:1 Tim 2:1-8; Gospel: Luke 16:1-13

There is a thoroughly modern ring about the life and times of Amos the prophet who lived in the eight century BC. Amos received a call from God to leave his flock and preach justice to the well-to-do people of Israel at a time of great national prosperity. However, it was also a period of great social unrest, with society sharply divided between the rich and the poor. Merchants were ruled by their hunger for profit while the poor were exploited and neglected. Amos condemned the sharp practice of dealers working the market and obtaining wealth at the expense of the poor and the needy whom they trampled upon and regarded as a commodity worth no more than a pair of sandals. In the present passage Amos bluntly denounces the unscrupulous traders for their false piety because they regard religious festivals and the Sabbath day of rest as wasted opportunities for wheeling and dealing, swindling and tampering, as well as all types of financial wizardry and fraudulent activity. Speaking frankly and critically he makes the point that religion and greed are poles apart, and that worship of God which does not influence the way people behave is false. Also, God is not deceived by their dishonest business practices and will punish them for their unscrupulous behaviour.

The message of Amos is still relevant in the world of today, as we are part of a society which is organised, not for the welfare of ordinary citizens, but as a component of a huge global economy. We live in a free enterprise system where everything is geared towards maximum production with profit for big business and the privileged few who can afford to invest in it. The one and only aim of the culture is the making of more and more money. On this road to economic affluence, nothing apart from the market seems to matter and human worth is measured in terms of spending power. Those who monopolise wealth, knowledge and power take advantage of their position to defend their privileges. The rich are enriched due to the impoverishment of the masses. The poor are manipulated without any thought given to concern for their well-being. More and more wealth is going to fewer and fewer and more and more people are getting poorer and poorer. While the tin gods of fame, power and success are great for those who win, they are hell for those who lose.

The gospel makes the point that we are but stewards of creation and that everything is given to us on trust and for safe-keeping. All is on loan, our tenure is brief and we are held accountable for our management. In a world of limited resources we cannot afford to squander our environment and are called to live responsibly, using what we need and sharing what we can. Material goods, which are necessary for life, are meant to be shared and it is decidedly immoral for a portion of the earth to become wealthy at the expense of the poorer parts. In achieving material abundance we have lost sight of our moral and spiritual bearings. Otherwise, how can it be that in the midst of plenty there are still people dying of hunger, condemned to illiteracy, lacking the most basic medical care and without a roof over their heads? The scenario of poverty is so widespread that we all tend to feel overwhelmed and rendered powerless by the magnitude of the problem. Nevertheless each of us can make a difference and we have a duty to do what we can to improve life for at least a few.

One of the worst features of our society is the prominence it gives to wealth. Even those who are not rich tend to make a God out of wealth. We are tinged with the Lotto mentality of getting rich quickly and think that winning a fortune would solve all our problems, put an end to worry and usher us into a life of ease and comfort. Our world seems to scream out that money is power and often we are all too ready to believe it. We need money to keep the roof over our heads and the wolf away from the door. Nevertheless, it is a ruthless ruler and has a way of enslaving us. Time spent acquiring it leaves little space in our heart for prayer and lesser opportunities for the exercise of Christian charity. When our days on earth run out, what will count is the person that we have become in the course of living. If we imitate Jesus, who spent his life serving the poor, the sick and the neglected, we are storing up treasures for ourselves in heaven.

Prayer of the Faithful

With unfailing love and confidence we bring our needs and concerns before our heavenly Father who wills the blessings of the earth to be shared and enjoyed by all humankind.

1. For all who bear responsibility in the church of Christ, that in their preaching, they promote a just social order and a fair distribution of wealth so that developing countries may also enjoy the blessings God has given us.
    Lord, hear us.

2. For those in local government, that they may not use their position of influence for their own selfish advancement but be generous in their response to the needs of the poor and marginalised in the community.
    Lord, hear us.

3. That in our country the values of kindness and concern may replace the harsh and selfish attitude of materialism and greed in the hearts of our people.
    Lord, hear us.

4. May we recognise the person of Jesus when he comes to us in the guise of the sick, the poor, the lonely and those who live daily with the knowledge of their approaching death.
    Lord, hear us.

5. We pray for those who have died, that the Lord may grant them the light of his kingdom in heaven.
    Lord, hear us.

Father, we thank you for the many gifts and blessings we receive from you day after day. Teach us to understand your will so that we may come to a full knowledge of the truth through Christ, our Lord. Amen.

26th Sunday in Ordinary Time
First Reading: Amos 6:1, 4-7;
Second Reading: 1 Tim 6:11-16; Gospel: Luke 16:19-31

Nothing attracts our attention more than a good story about real
life with which we can identify. The street setting of the beggar
at the rich man's gateway with no company but that of the scav-
enging dogs licking his sores, evokes our sympathy. Time has
not rendered such scenes obsolete for it is a picture we have become accustomed to, as it fills our television screens and newspapers day after day. Lazarus is all around us, not as an appari-
tion from another world but in the pitiful spectres of humanity
who aimlessly walk our city streets, doss down in doorways and
constitute the underclass in our midst. They tend to become a
shadowy background feature of city life that nobody notices.
This scene of unspeakable destitution, which is in stark contrast
to Dives basking in the lap of luxury, eating sumptuously and
flaunting his wealth, is no exaggeration. Squalor in the presence
of splendour has always been part of the human landscape.
Lazarus lies in misery at the gates of plenty. The poor exist but
don't count.

This is a parable about justice for the poor and a challenge to
reach out to them. What is more important to Jesus than wealth
or poverty is whether people care for one another. There is nothing in the story to suggest that Dives ill-treated Lazarus, was
rude to him, shouted obscenities after him, held him in contempt or had him removed from his gate. It is not so much
wealth that is the problem as the failure of Dives to notice
Lazarus. He is faulted for his indifference to the poor man's
plight. Dives was so preoccupied with his pleasures and his
high life that he was unaware of the beggar's presence, never
mind the sharing of a crust of bread with him. His self-centred
behaviour of keeping himself to himself is appalling and totally
reprehensible. The rich man's sin was in what he failed to do. He
never as much as lifted a finger to help Lazarus in his dire distress. He is not condemned for being rich but is damned for
doing nothing when he should have been doing something.
Here we can see ourselves in the story. This is where we fit into

the picture. We are all called to share what we have with the poor. What about the times we could have given something to charity and just did nothing at all? Sins of omission are all too easily overlooked.

We live in a world where there is a dreadful split between the wealthy and the deprived. It is highly regrettable that with all our technical knowledge the vast majority of people are deprived of their fair share of human life. The cause of poverty is difficult to label but its consequences are merciless and cruel. Half the world is dying of hunger amidst an abundance of full and plenty. The greed and selfishness of the rich man's club have slammed the door of the good life and left many third world countries hurting, grieving and facing starvation. Our world is too small to bear such inequalities. Given the magnitude of the problem of global misery the temptation for many is one of despair. Nevertheless, the fact that we cannot do everything is not an excuse for doing nothing at all. Nations are beginning to realise that this world was given to us as a gift. It has to be cared for and is not something that can be ravaged at will. If we cannot combine the fight for a better environment with the fight against poverty, we cannot blame the people in Africa for cutting down a tree when they have no fuel.

As Christians our vocation in life is to proclaim the dignity of every human person and to be at the service of the poor and needy. We have got to seek out ways in which we become a voice for the voiceless because the poor of the world are our brothers and sisters. It can only be right that we stand up and care for those who are in great need. We must never be content to leave them on the breadline. If we have a surplus of anything then we should share. Let us remember that it is in giving that we receive. The poor provide us with an opportunity of opening our hearts and practising charity. Lazarus was the rich man's sole opportunity of shaping his eternal destiny for the better. He was the only lifeline to help Dives place himself within the range of God's grace. Dives failed to avail of the offer and his life ended in torment.

Prayer of the Faithful

Challenged to change our lives and to put ourselves at the service of the deprived so that true justice may reign in the world we turn to God the Father with our prayers and petitions, knowing that he will favourably hear our request.

1. That the church in its preaching and teaching may have a commitment to social justice in order to show forth the compassion of Christ to those who are poor, downtrodden and oppressed.
   Lord, hear us.

2. That those who govern the country may not be blinded by materialism and selfish gain but work to attain greater equality among people.
   Lord, hear us.

3. That the prosperous nations of the world may learn to share their riches with the poor who sit patiently at the closed doors of life's banquet.
   Lord, hear us.

4. We ask God to strengthen with his loving presence, the sick, the dying and those who experience poverty and pain.
   Lord, hear us.

5. For those who have recently died: may they share with Lazarus the happiness and peace of God's kingdom.
   Lord, hear us.

Heavenly Father, give us the grace to treat all our brothers and sisters with compassion and so build up the kingdom of justice, love and peace which Jesus came on earth to establish. We ask this through Christ, our Lord. Amen.

27th Sunday in Ordinary Time
First Reading: Habakkuk 1:2-3, 2:2-4 ;
Second Reading: 2 Tim 1:6-8, 13-14; Gospel: Luke 17:5-10

When tragedy strikes, the questions most people ask are, 'Where is God in the midst of all this?' 'How can he allow such happenings to take place?' 'Could this catastrophe not have been averted by divine intervention?' There is nothing new about these questions, for they have exercised great minds throughout history. While the problem is acknowledged and confronted, there are no convincing answers given. Almost three thousand years ago as the Babylonian army was surrounding the city of Jerusalem with a ring of steel, the prophet Habakkuk screams out to God in desperation at the predicament of his people. He accuses the Lord of abandoning his flock and simply looking on as tyranny and violence flourish. It seems that God has turned a deaf ear to his anguish and Habakkuk laments bitterly at what appears to be the Lord's indifference to the most horrible atrocities. Everywhere evil triumphs and the wicked get the better of the upright. Habakkuk expresses his dismay at the distress of the downtrodden people and demands that God intervene. When God finally makes his presence felt it is with a vision and not with an answer. The prophet is assured that his desperate plea will not go unheeded for in God's good time the proud will be punished. Through the ebb and flow of history, God is in charge. In the meantime Habakkuk and everyone else will have to wait in faith until the appointed time arrives.

All too often we expect life to be nice and smooth and hope God will reward us for our good behaviour, as well as show up when we really need him. The truth is that we would like to control God, to try and win him over to our way of thinking, to whittle his actions down to what fits in with our shallow domestic designs for the world. We forget that God is awesome mystery and does not act in the ways or schedules of humans. The psalmist tells us that God's ways are not our ways; his plans are not our plans. He owes us nothing and certainly does not come to offer a quick fix to our problems nor a happy release from what is bothering us. As the gospel says: 'When we have done all we are supposed to do, we are unprofitable servants who have done no more than our duty.'

While times of near despair are no respecter of age or gender, nevertheless, a setback or a crisis can focus the mind and make us realise what matters most in life. These are the moments when we stand before the twin doorways of faith and despair trying desperately to decide through which door we shall pass. Whatever else is achieved, inessentials are certainly sorted out.

The gospel stresses the importance of unwavering faith, which is the courage to live with the uncertainty of not knowing all the answers. Often it is having the strength to live with the questions that keep bothering us. Jesus seems to be saying that we have more faith than we credit ourselves with. He stresses the importance of putting that faith into action because we are a fragment and a seedling of God's presence in the world and are capable of performing wondrous things. Like the stars, the grace of God is there in the life of everyone, whether they know it or not.

Faith does make a difference in the way we view our life and makes it possible to carry many a cross that would otherwise seem insupportable. It is never a question of faith or no faith; the question always is 'In what or in whom do I put my faith?' – possessions, power, people, or God. People of faith believe that every person matters and that God takes small things and makes them into great things. As we take to heart the word of God, faith can inspire us to change direction and accomplish marvellous feats. It tells us that we don't have to accept things the way they are. Faith is knowing without seeing, believing without fully understanding and trusting without touching the One who is ever faithful. Faith is when we step out and do the things we believe God wants us to do, even if it doesn't make sense.

Having created the natural world, God has placed us as stewards of his creation. He has left us free to create the social world and it is up to us to build or destroy, to hurt or heal, to reach out or remain selfish.

Prayer of the Faithful

Aware of our weaknesses and failures we turn now to our heavenly Father, who holds our future is in his hands, and ask him for an increase in grace.

1. For those involved in the ministry of the church: may they communicate the message of Christ convincingly by all they say and do.
   Lord, hear us.

2. That we may appreciate the gift of faith that has been handed on to us and pass it on so that others may find hope in the Christian message.
   Lord, hear us.

3. For those assailed by doubts or weighed down by uncertainties and who are wavering in their religious conviction: may they not grow despondent but have the courage and strength to persevere.
   Lord, hear us.

4. We pray that all those who struggle with illness may experience the healing power of God.
   Lord, hear us.

5. We commend to God's care those who have died and have gone before us marked with the sign of faith. May they be given eternal rest.
   Lord, hear us.

Loving Creator, look upon your people in their need and support us with your blessing. Teach us to be courageous and trusting. Grant us faithfulness in all things through Christ, our Lord. Amen.

28th Sunday in Ordinary Time
First Reading: 2 Kings 5: 14-17;
Second Reading: 2 Tim 2: 8-13; Gospel: Luke 17:11-19

College students studying Shakespeare's play 'King Lear' are always amazed at the ingratitude and cruelty of the king's two monstrous daughters who added nastiness and malice to their lack of thanks. King Lear's cry of sorrow, 'How sharper than a serpent's tooth it is to have a thankless child', repeats itself across the world and down the years. As small children when we listened to the story of Cinderella, the ingratitude and hardness of the ugly sisters stunned us. It all goes to show that saying thanks does not come naturally to us but is something we have to learn. The instinct of parents is properly directed when it seeks to instil in very young children the habit of saying 'Thank you.' How often do we hear parents asking their children, Did you say 'Thank you'? after they have received a gift from a relative or a friend. It is one of the first lessons a child has to put into practice after learning how to talk.

In the course of everyday life many of us are willing to make generous sacrifices of time, energy, or money for others for no higher reward than a simple 'Thank you'. We may hasten to reply 'Don't mention it' but nevertheless, we still like to be recognised for favours and gifts rendered which are over and above the call of duty. Few vices irritate us more than the trait of ingratitude, which is one of the least attractive of human characteristics. More than likely we have experienced going out of our way to help someone without so much as an acknowledgement or a word of appreciation for our efforts. It has left us with a bitter taste as well as the lament, 'I did this, that and the other, and there was never a word of thanks.' When gratitude isn't shown, we are often left feeling puzzled and disappointed.

There is no story in the scriptures which so poignantly points out human ingratitude as that of the ten lepers who came to Jesus with a desperate longing to be cured of their loathsome disease. They begged for mercy but when the crisis passed saw things differently. Jesus was tapping deeply into ordinary human emotions when he uttered those heartbreak words:

'Were not ten made clean? The other nine, where are they?' He was obviously bothered by their lack of appreciation. We might well wonder what was the reason for such a display of ungratefulness. What makes people that way? Why is saying 'Thank you' such a problem? Maybe the lepers were so excited at being back in society that they clean forgot the one who heard their cry of distress and cured them. Perhaps they thought that Jesus was just doing his job as a healer and took their cure for granted. Could it be that they resented the fact that they needed help? Whatever the reason, their display of ingratitude diminished them as individuals. What is more, they missed the deep inner peace and joy that comes from giving thanks.

Thankfulness is not a once-off response for favours received but an attitude of soul that is always ready to give thanks because it regards everything in life as a gift. It springs from a heart that acknowledges that we are touched by grace from countless sources. God is an endless source of benediction. At every eucharistic celebration we say, 'Let us give thanks to the Lord Our God', and we declare it the proper thing to do, recognising that there is so much in life to be thankful for. There is the fruitful earth that provides us with nourishment. There is the beauty and majesty of sea and sky, mountain and rivers. Like St Francis, we can praise and thank God for sun and moon and stars, for flowers and trees, for animals and birds and for our life and health and strength that comes from him alone. We who are well and enjoy good health have as much reason to thank God as the lepers who received a miraculous cure. A clean skin, the gift of sight and speech, of health of body and mind are no less wonderful because we enjoy them everyday. When we are feeling well and healthy it is easy to forget to say thanks. Let's take time out today to express our gratitude to family and friends for their many kindnesses to us and for standing by us when we needed help.

O God, you have given so much to me;
Give me one thing more, a grateful heart.

Prayer of the Faithful

Aware of our need for wholeness we come before the Lord, trusting in his unfailing love for sinners and make our prayer.

1. We pray that the leaders of the church, guided by the Spirit, may preach by example and lead their people into the footsteps of Christ.
   Lord, hear us.

2. May we find time to deepen our sense of gratitude for the health we enjoy and may we never take for granted the countless signs of God's presence in our lives.
   Lord, hear us.

3. May we be sensitive to the needs of people around us and always recognise God's presence in the poor and disadvantaged.
   Lord, hear us.

4. For the sick and the handicapped, that they may experience the healing touch of Christ.
   Lord, hear us.

5. We pray for the dead, especially our friends and relatives who have left this world and returned to God. May they enter into his kingdom of love and eternal happiness.
   Lord, hear us.

Heavenly Father, teach us to be always grateful for the many good things you have given us. Keep us true to the life you share with us. Make us aware of the needs of other people. We make this prayer through Christ, our Lord. Amen.

29th Sunday in Ordinary Time
First Reading: Exodus 17:8-13;
Second Reading: 2 Tim 3:14-4:2; Gospel: Luke 18:1-8

When the Israelites made good their escape from slavery in Egypt their troubles were far from over. No sooner had they left Pharaoh's armies behind than a new enemy, the Amalekites, a nomadic tribe, who roamed the Sinai desert and controlled the caravan route between Arabia and Egypt, confronted them. The bible records a long history of hostility between these two peoples. In olden times, wars were generally fought over land or resources, which were essential for a people to survive. The battle reported here, raged over the control of desert watering holes and pasturage for animals. The Israelites were no match for the superior forces of the Amalekites who were very much at home in the terrain of the wilderness. The only thing that prevented an Israelite defeat was the intervention of Moses. We have a colourful scene of Joshua and his fighting men struggling on the battlefield while Moses was on the mountaintop with arms outstretched in prayer. As long as Moses kept his hands raised and held high the staff of Yahweh, the Israelites prevailed but when his arms grew weary and he experienced moments of confusion and doubt the enemy advanced. Supported by Aaron and Hur, Moses held up his arms all day long in constant prayer until victory was assured. The story illustrates the absolute importance of persevering and remaining faithful in prayer even against what appears to be impossible odds.

In the course of life many of us have experienced the disappointment that comes from praying for all sorts of things that were never granted. We have prayed for loved ones in failing health that they might be spared the burden of extreme suffering, only to witness them dying inch by inch. Then there was the job that we had our heart set on which never materialised. We are on bended knees this many a year hoping for a let-up over Johnny's drinking but things only seem to be getting progressively worse. The evidence is all around that praying does not save loved ones from misery and death. Nothing is more difficult than to keep on praying under such circumstances and especially when nothing seems to be happening. The list of unanswered prayers is endless so it is small wonder that we lose heart and stop praying. We forget that prayer does not always result in a request granted. While God does not answer every prayer precisely as we would wish, he does answer persistent prayer in a way that is advantageous to us. God is not in a hurry and responds to prayer in his own time and in his own way. There is a gospel song that teaches, 'He may not be there when you want him, but the Lord, he's always right on time.' We may have to wait years for his response and when it does come about it may be in a way far different from what we expected. It can also happen that a lot of the time we pray for the impossible to take place forgetting that God does not hand out miracles.

Prayer has enormous power but to experience that power we must develop the strength of character to deal with disappointments and not expect immediate results. We need to have the perseverance of the widow in today's gospel who had been wronged, robbed of her rights, pushed aside and ignored. She is faced with a ruthless judge who is no respecter of God or man, who treats her like dirt and can't be bothered hearing her case. However, she has nerve, she has endurance and in spite of repeated rejections she keeps on pestering the judge. Giving up her struggle, letting go, or taking no for an answer are the last things on her mind. She proves herself to be more than a match for the judge who has no option but to cave in and grant her request. Her persistence wins the day. Jesus holds her up as an example of how we should storm heaven with our prayers until our wishes are granted.

Living as we do in a society, which demands instant gratification for all our needs, and where everything is geared to take the waiting out of wanting, we often expect God to give an immediate answer to our calls. The fact that ours is an age where nothing is meant to last and where everything is disposable makes us less prepared to persevere. Prayer is being in touch with God. A daily habit of prayer is a way of showing God that we are serious about our relationship with him. It brings us closer to God and begins the process of allowing God to fill us with himself. It is the source of our spiritual nourishment and helps us acknowledge our dependence on the Lord.

Prayer of the Faithful

With unlimited confidence in God's unfailing love we pray now for our own needs and for those of the church.

1. We pray for those who exercise authority and power in the church, that they may be motivated to serve those in their care with reverence and love.
   Lord, hear us.

2. For those in our area who are poor and are in any way disadvantaged. May our eyes be open to see their needs and our arms outstretched to offer help.
   Lord, hear us.

3. That we may continue to persevere praying in faith and love even when God seems absent and we are in danger of losing heart.
   Lord, hear us.

4. We pray for the sick and those who are lonely, anxious and afraid, that they may experience the consolation and the healing power of Christ.
   Lord, hear us.

5. We pray for the dead. May the Lord have mercy on them and bring them to eternal life.
   Lord, hear us.

Gracious and loving God, we entrust to you the burden of our needs. Teach us fidelity and simplicity in prayer, especially in times when we are discouraged. Help us to come closer to you. Keep us always in your grace through Christ, our Lord. Amen.

30th Sunday in Ordinary Time
First Reading: Sirach 35:12-14, 16-19;
Second Reading: 2 Timothy 4:6-8, 16-18; Gospel: Luke 18:9-14

When Jesus walked the dusty roads of Palestine he came in contact with all types of people. Some were highly respectable God-
fearing members of society but the vast majority were ordinary
folk who were lacking in a sense of self worth and regarded
themselves as sinners and of no consequence. The Pharisee and
the tax collector at prayer in the temple typify such an encounter
and challenges us to draw our own conclusions from the story.
Brimming with self-confidence the Pharisee addresses the Lord
and manages to use 'I' six times in the course of his short prayer.
We learn from his brief outburst of religious fervour that he is
generous and charitable, faithful and pious and that he fasts regularly. His prayer was just that little bit over the top for it
seemed he was boasting to God of how good a man he was.
However, had he not turned around and noticed the tax collector
at the back of the temple matters would not have got completely
out of hand. The sight of such an intruder in God's sacred space
brought out the worst in him. After all, here was one of those
hated classes, despised as loathsome lackeys of the Roman authorities who bled the poor of their money. What was such a
notorious public sinner doing in the temple? There was no
doubt that the Pharisee regarded himself as the perfect example
of how a true Jewish religious believer should worship. It never
occurred to him that in his prayer he was bragging, acting smug
and lest he forgot, was gently reminding God of his outstanding
spiritual achievements. What a contrast he was to the tax collector who was unsure of his right to be there but, with shamed
face and bowed head, knew his place before God. The tax collector was painfully aware, not of the height of his virtue, but of the
weight of his sins. He has nothing to offer God but his own
wrongdoing and brokenness. Not even daring to come forward,
he stays at the back, bows humbly before his God, admits his
faults, beats his breast and in the depth of distress mutters his
plea for forgiveness: 'O God, be merciful to me a sinner.'

We feel good when we learn that the tax collector's prayer of repentance wins acceptance before God and that he goes home with a blessing. What dominates his attitude more than anything else is the recognition of his sinfulness. It's an example of the humble man's prayer piercing the clouds and getting straight to the heart of God. Secretly we are delighted that the Pharisee has got his comeuppance. None of us likes the insufferable Holy Joes in our midst who make a virtue out of parading their religion, as well as being able to catalogue every good act that they ever performed in the course of their entire life. The parable forcibly illustrates that people who are highly respected members of society are not always people who are at rights with God, so let's not get hung up on externals. It also makes it clear that pride does not walk humbly with God and that no one should be looked down on, held in contempt or despised. Spiritual pride loves attention, thrives on recognition and demands affirmation because it is self-centred and not God centred. It forgets that God's grace and blessing are free gifts and cannot be earned or merited. We need to remember that any good in our lives comes from God through the saving work of Jesus on the cross.

The world around us is full of grades, scores and statistics, which we use to take our measure against one and other. Much sadness and unhappiness flows directly from such comparisons, and most of this comparing is useless and an utter waste of time. While we like to identify with the tax collector in the gospel, if the truth were known there are streaks of the Pharisee in our make-up. When we boast that our children are better behaved than the family down the street, or that we can drink in moderation unlike the yahoos who waken the neighbourhood with their late night weekend revelry and never darken the door of the church, we are coming perilously close to identifying with the Pharisee. In this gospel Jesus cautions against contempt, snobbery and thinking ourselves better than our neighbour. Our station in life does not impress him in the least. He knows who and what we are. We are all sinners and deeply in need of opening our hearts to his merciful love.

Prayer of the Faithful

As sinners in need of forgiveness, we come before the Father who has loved us from the first moment of our existence, lay open our lives and ask for his blessing.

1. For all who exercise the service of leadership in the church, that they may lead humble and Christ-like lives.
   Lord, hear us.

2. Help us to listen to the cry of the poor and have the courage to do what we can to help them.
   Lord, hear us.

3. For our local community, that we may shun the pride of the Pharisee and never parade our good deeds, nor look down with disdain on other people, but be attentive to their plight.
   Lord, hear us.

4. For those in the caring professions and for all who are working selflessly to bring comfort to the sick, that they may experience joy and fulfilment in their work.
   Lord, hear us.

5. We ask the Lord to give peace to all who have died, particularly those who have no one on earth to pray for them.
   Lord, hear us.

Heavenly Father, accept our prayers on behalf of the whole church. Through this celebration of the Eucharist may we learn to serve you faithfully and to draw closer to you with thanks and love. We make our prayer through Christ, our Lord. Amen.

31st Sunday in Ordinary Time
First Reading: Wisdom 11:22-12:2;
Second Reading: 2 Thessalonians 1:11-2:2; Gospel: Luke 19:1-10

I never cease to be amazed at the ever-increasing size of Sunday
newspapers. Every topic under the sun that will make the jour-
nal interesting and marketable is included. One particular paper
has a section called 'The Funday Times' which is geared to appeal to the younger members of the household. Reading this
light-hearted gospel story of Zacchaeus makes me wonder was
this the type of approach Christ used for teaching and getting
his message across when there were children in the gathering?
This action-packed gospel story has all the ingredients necessary
for the making of a good comic strip.

Zacchaeus is very short and stubby. Nobody likes him or
wants to be in his company for he is a tax collector, a cheat, a
swindler and a bully. He bleeds the poor of their every penny.
You can imagine the scene as Jesus enters the gates of Jericho.
Everybody swarms around, anxious to get a glimpse of the wandering preacher, the miracle man from Nazareth. Zacchaeus is
no different for he too is anxious to meet Jesus because there is
something terribly wrong in his life. He has no friends and is
desperately lonely. His wealth has not brought him happiness.
Riches are no protection against his inner pain. He bobs up and
down on his tiptoes trying to get a glance of Jesus but to no avail
for he is small of stature and the crowd pushes him into the
background. Nevertheless, Zacchaeus persists in his desire to
reach Jesus and, not to be outdone, runs ahead of the crowd,
scurries up a sycamore tree and plants himself on one of the
branches.

On passing by Jesus spots Zacchaeus, calls him by name and
beckons him to come down from his lonely perch. 'Zacchaeus,
come down, hurry because I must stay at your house today.'
Jesus doesn't lay down the law or point out how big a sinner he
is. He simply calls him by name and Zacchaeus responds, comes
down immediately and welcomes Jesus as his guest.

Being accepted by Jesus makes all the difference to
Zacchaeus. He is deeply moved at being loved and having the

hand of friendship extended. His heart is touched in a profound way and he becomes a changed man. What's more he is able to repent of his wrongdoing as well as pledging to respond generously in his compensation.

However, the crowd is shocked for they would have regarded Zacchaeus as beyond redemption. No self-respecting Jew would dare be seen in his company. For Jesus to openly associate with such a sinner was to invite fury and horror as well as calling into question his claim to be a man of God. Under their breath the crowd start to mutter, does Jesus not care about the company he keeps? Is he only interested in outcasts? Little did they realise that when Jesus was mixing with social outcasts like Zacchaeus, he was making the point that nobody is excluded from the mercy and kindness of God. It was his way of showing that God's love and forgiveness is a free gift that is open to everybody, no matter who they are or what harm they may have done.

The story of Zacchaeus is a powerful example of God's forgiving love at work in the world. It demonstrates that no person or situation is beyond hope or outside the limits of God's mercy. When we hurt all over, live in a shame we can't bear, and are on our knees because of the weight of our sins and in our helplessness beg forgiveness for our wrongdoing, it is then that we leave ourselves open for the power of God to get to work in our lives. Christ's invitation to Zacchaeus to hurry is addressed to everyone here present who is not happy with their situation. This is an opportunity to open our hearts and place before God our fears, our worries, our uncertainties and to ask for the richness of his healing presence in the midst of our concerns. He reaches out to us as he did to Zacchaeus in total acceptance. Jesus is always out and about meeting people, befriending them where they are and offering them a love that has the power to change their lives. It is a love that involves continuous conversion and a change of behaviour on our part. Knowing that we are accepted unconditionally by God should lead us to respond generously too. We have a future and should not be held back by our sinful past.

Prayer of the Faithful

Aware of our need to be healed of the hurts inflicted by our sinfulness we acknowledge our weaknesses and shortcomings in the presence of our merciful Father.

1. For the leaders of our church that that they may take their inspiration from Christ and become channels of God's mercy and forgiveness.
   Lord, hear us.

2. That those who inflict injury and hurt on the innocent through ignorance, fear or prejudice, may open their eyes to the error of their ways and so change their lives.
   Lord, hear us.

3. For all who have turned away from God through pride, permissiveness and the desire for pleasure and wealth; make them aware of their sinfulness and help them realise that only in you is true happiness to be found.
   Lord, hear us.

4. Send your blessing on the sick, the needy, the deprived and all who stand in need of your loving care.
   Lord, hear us.

5. That those who have died may know the peace and joy of being with God.
   Lord, hear us.

God of goodness and love, fill our hearts with the spirit of repentance which will lead us to true peace. Guide us in holiness and help us spend our lives in your service. We make our prayer through Christ, our Lord. Amen.

32nd Sunday in Ordinary Time
First Reading: 2 Maccabees 7:1-2, 9-14;
Second Reading: 2 Thessalonians 2:16-3:5; Gospel: Luke 20:27-38

On a visit to Norwich Cathedral last year I was somewhat taken aback by a plaque on the wall which caught my eye. It was an epitaph in memory of a man called Thomas Gooding who lived some four hundred years ago. The inscription read:

All you that do this plaque pass by,
Remember death, for you must die,
As you are now, even so was I
And as I am, so shall ye be.
Thomas Gooding here to stay,
Waiting for God's judgement day.

The one thing that we can all be sure of is the inevitability of death. As we grow older, we realise more clearly that death is not just something that happens in the life of other people but a personal appointment that we must all keep. The frailty and vulnerability of life makes us more aware of things spiritual. Waiting for God's judgement day is a reminder of the serious nature of life's pilgrimage. The death of a friend or a family member can stir up feelings of grief and anger at the loss of someone so close. It can cause people to stop their normal life to consider more fundamental questions like why am I here? And what is the purpose of my life? The month of November is a fitting time to do some serious thinking on this aspect of our faith. It is the time of year when growth has ceased. The days are damp, the trees are bare, the weather is cooler and the nights are long. Nature seems to be preaching its own silent sermon about the end of things. This is the time the church sets aside for Christians to remember those who have gone before them – family members, friends, neighbours – those who have died recently and those who have died in the distant past. So many friends and relatives gone to the grave, rounded the corner on the road to eternity, whose lives shaped our character and contributed to the very stuff of our being. Their passing has swelled our souls with grief. They may have passed from our sight but the bonds of friendship between them and us remain constant. They continue to walk and talk with us and their influence is still felt in our midst. The one thing that the human heart longs for most is to be remembered. There is never a parting, never a farewell without the words, don't forget, remember to call, write a letter, keep in touch. To be remembered means that one's existence extends beyond physical reality. When we remember the dead, particularly in November, their names, personalities and stories live on. We have our own ways of keeping those memories alive. For some it is the laying of a wreath, the celebrating of an anniversary, visiting a grave, writing a name on a dead list. For others it is the lighting of a candle, the glance at a photograph on a mantelpiece or a quiet moment in prayer as a name springs to mind. We remember in a special way those with whom we have lovingly passed happy times, those who shared our childhood or were part of our early adult years. There is a tug of the heart and we hold back a tear as we think of the love and sacrifices parents poured out for our sakes. All those memories are part of the broad landscape of our lives and they are something we find consoling and strengthening.

Remembering our dead can mean much more than praying for them. It brings home to all of us that we too must pass over the threshold of death to our judgement. Then we will be asked to answer for all our deeds. Our downfall may not be the wrong doings we feel bad about. Our sins of omission and our failure to perform good works and live the gospel message may weigh more heavily against us than our own personal shortcomings.

Jesus' words in today's gospel are reassuring, as they remind us that death is not the end, for we believe in a God, not of the dead but of the living. To remember family and friends is to show love and express concern. Ever since the first Good Friday on the Hill of Calvary when the repentant thief cried out from one cross to another: 'Lord, remember me, when you come into your kingdom,' this prayerful holding of people in mind and in heart has been at the centre of the life of the church. Our belief is that we shall all meet again, and that those who live in the Lord never see each other for the last time.

Prayer of the Faithful

We make our prayer to God the Father whose word brings us comfort and a sure hope throughout our lives.

1. For the church, that the faith of its members may show forth the light of hope to all in the world who are in darkness.
   Lord, hear us.

2. That those who live without hope may come to know Christ and to believe in the eternal life he has promised.
   Lord, hear us.

3. We pray for all those who work in hospice care and those tending the sick and the dying: that the compassion of God may shine through their work.
   Lord, hear us.

4. May the good Lord comfort all whose spirit is crushed and who are broken hearted at the death of a loved one.
   Lord, hear us.

5. We pray that those who have died may share with the angels the glory of the Lord.
   Lord, hear us.

Heavenly Father, your only-begotten Son conquered death and won eternal life for us. Grant that all who believe may overcome death and share in his glory, through Christ, our Lord. Amen.

33rd Sunday in Ordinary Time
First Reading: Malachi 3: 19-20;
Second Reading: 2 Thess 3:7-12; Gospel: Luke 21:5-19

One of the wonders of the ancient Jewish world was the Temple in Jerusalem. This sacred spot, which was a symbol of the abiding presence of God amongst the chosen people, was an architectural gem and the pride and glory of Israel. It was a centre of pilgrimage and a visit to this hallowed site was something every devout Jew hoped to make in the course of a lifetime. During his final visit to the temple, shortly before his passion and death, Jesus shocked the onlookers who were remarking on the magnificence of the building by making a prediction that the day would arrive when everything would be destroyed. 'All these things you are staring at now – the time will come when not a single stone will be left on another.' The idea of the Temple with all its grandeur being reduced to a pile of rubble was unthinkable and was not the kind of message his audience wanted to hear. It beggared belief that this most holy sanctuary could ever cease to exist.

Further grim listening comes when he predicts the doomsday scenario of destruction, utter chaos and confusion that will herald the end of the world. The Day of the Lord, as it is called, will be a time when the faithful will endure extreme hardship and suffer persecution for their beliefs. However, no matter what trials and tribulations come their way, they must remain calm and steady, as there is no need to be afraid because God is always present to comfort and strengthen them.

The bible reserves some of its richest pictorial language to describe the end of the world and there is a certain measure of ambiguity and mystery in describing this time. We have every right to be wary of fire and brimstone preachers with their dire warnings and inaccurate predictions of disaster, which are calculated to instil fear into the bravest of hearts. However, there is no uncertainty about the coming of the Lord that we will all experience with death, and we had better get ready for it. As we grow older, we come to realise the brevity of our human existence. Everything passes. Life as we know it will fade away.

Within a limited number of years each of us will face death. Paul reminds the people of Thessalonica that idleness is no way to prepare for this event but that they should go on quietly working. Whatever the future brings, the inescapable fact is that Christ speaks emphatically about judgement. All of us are on the road leading to judgement and there is no reason to presume it to be merely a matter of formality. We cannot sit back and take our salvation for granted. The gospel states that entry into the kingdom will be by a narrow gate and will demand genuine effort on our part. It will be a case of struggling rather than strolling in. The Lord will come to set all things right on what will be a personal day of reckoning for the just and the unjust alike. If our lives have been lived up to this moment with selfish indifference, now is the time to put things right.

The end of the church year, with the gloom of winter upon us, is a good time to do some thinking about life in all its dimensions. We can be so caught up in our present existence that we lose sight of our eternal destiny. The pursuit of a career, the lure of riches and the achieving of short-term human ambitions can dominate us to such an extent that our horizons are limited solely to this world. We can end up an empty person with an uneasy inner feeling that our total absorption in the world of work is not what life is all about. To gain a deeper perspective on the values of life, we need to take time to reflect on: Why am I here? What is the purpose of my being alive and of my existence in this world? What do I hope for from living? Where is my pilgrim journey taking me? What message might God be conveying to me through these words from sacred scripture?

The last line of the gospel announces triumphantly that there will be a new life with God for those who endure in the name of Christ. It stresses the importance of keeping faith and not losing heart. God calls us, not to success but to faithfulness. If we endure in our efforts to become loving persons who are respectful of other people, our lives will have all the meaning and purpose that is necessary. We need have no fear. It is God's world, he is in control and things will unfold in accordance with his plan.

Prayer of the Faithful

We make our prayer to the Father who is the same yesterday, today and forever and who desires all people to be saved and come to a knowledge of the truth.

1. We pray for the leaders of the church. May the Lord give them an eloquence and a wisdom to guide the church on its pilgrim way in the midst of a confused and chaotic world. Lord, hear us.

2. We pray for strength of purpose and endurance as we struggle to cope with the problems of daily life. Lord, hear us.

3. We pray for those who work hard for their living. May they find joy and fulfilment in their employment. Lord, hear us.

4. We pray for the sick and all those troubled in mind and spirit that they may find hope and encouragement in God's promises. Lord, hear us.

5. We pray for all who have departed this life. May the day of the Lord be for them a day of rejoicing and gladness. Lord, hear us.

Heavenly Father, keep us always in your care. Through our celebration of this Eucharist help us to live in the world guided by the values of the gospel and so attain a place in your kingdom. We make our prayer through Christ, our Lord, Amen.

34th Sunday in Ordinary Time
The Feast of Christ the King
First Reading: 2 Samuel 5:1-3;
Second Reading: Col 1:11-20; Gospel: Luke 23: 35-43

This gospel, which is the grand finale of our liturgical year, recalls that first Good Friday scene with a snapshot of a hillside outside the walls of Jerusalem where three men are hanging on crosses. It is an angry and emotional setting and all eyes are focused on Jesus, the Holy Man from Galilee who is being crucified between two commonplace criminals. This is his hour of abject disgrace and utter humiliation. One thief, with an amazing arrogance for a man so close to death, is screeching blasphemies and hurling insults at him, while the other, touched by Christ's innocence, implores his favour and is immediately rewarded beyond his wildest dreams. The crowd standing around watch in sheer amazement while the soldiers, vesting Christ in the emblems of royalty with a purple cloak and a crown of thorns jeer, hurl abuse and fix a notice above his head with the scribbled inscription: 'King of the Jews'. Meanwhile the religious authorities, treating him as a blasphemer, mockingly taunt him to perform the spectacular, get off the cross and save himself. Amidst all this, Christ's only source of comfort is his mother and a few friends who stand there at the foot of the cross, faithful to the last.

In this crucifixion scene Luke highlights the merciful and compassionate role of Jesus. The thief who was pardoned on the cross was by no means an innocent, and yet his humble appeal, 'Jesus remember me when you come into your kingdom,' echoes down the centuries. His request was answered before eventide with the richest of all promises. The declaration, 'Indeed, I promise you, today you will be with me in paradise' are words we are all longing to hear. They capture the essence of Christ's eternal power to touch, convert and console the needy heart, and make him Saviour king of all who turn his way for help. On the cross Jesus won pardon not just for the repentant thief but also for you and me and for all lost souls and wandering sinners. The rest is up to us. To receive his mercy, all we have to do is to acknowledge our sinfulness, repent, implore his help and he will impart his grace into our being.

We live in democratic times and most nations have become disenchanted with royalty. The days are long gone when kings could claim royal authority as a divine right. Their manner of ruling and lording it over their subjects was a far cry from the humble man of Nazareth whose footsteps we trace in the gospel and who breathed his last between two robbers on the Hill of Calvary. Jesus is certainly unlike any other king, for his rule is not based on position, privilege or power but on the very high ideals of service, compassion and love. His ministry is one of healing and reconciling. The touching story of the repentant thief, who moves from despair and hopelessness to faith and promise, reaffirms Christ's desire to reign in the human heart.

This feast reminds us that the world needs to see Jesus and can only do so by the love and care we show to the poor and the neglected. It challenges us by our living out of gospel values, to make a clear statement of what we think of Christ who is inviting us at every moment to measure up to his standards and to answer his call wholeheartedly. To do so, will involve putting aside self-indulgence, vanity and pride so as to allow Jesus give direction to our lives. It will entail taking time out to listen to the stories of hurt from the heartbroken, the disappointed and the discouraged in order to assure them of their special place in God's kingdom.

If Christ the King is to be something more than a figurehead, we have to pledge ourselves in loving service to his way of life. We are invited to look forward to the day when his kingship over all things will be visible and full and will bring joy to the whole of creation. In the meantime we have got to realise that his kingdom begins here and now in our hearts and that the process of making all things new is taking place and growing quietly everyday through the lives we lead. The gospel is certainly thought provoking. It invites us to examine our lives in the light of the service we offer to Christ crucified who came to serve and give his life as a ransom for many. The celebration of the feast on the last Sunday of the church year signifies how things shall be at the end of the ages. Christ is the Lord of all. May his kingdom come!

Prayer of the Faithful

Trusting in the Father's continued care for his children, with faith and confidence we make our prayer for the church and for the world.

1. We pray for all who hold positions of leadership in the church: that they may guide the people of God in the ways of justice, love and peace.
   Lord, hear us.

2. We pray that all governing authorities in our land may use their power and influence with wisdom and integrity and show special concern for the weaker and disadvantaged members of society.
   Lord, hear us.

3. For peace in our homes and a restoration of harmony among those estranged from parents, partners and former friends.
   Lord, hear us.

4. That those who are sick or troubled may be comforted by those who care for them.
   Lord, hear us.

5. For those who have died. May they rejoice forever with Christ the King in paradise.
   Lord, hear us.

Lord God, guide and support of all that we have and are, may all our efforts on this pilgrim journey be directed to serving your Son. May he reign in our lives and so lead us to his eternal kingdom. We ask this through the same Christ, our Lord. Amen.

Feast of the Immaculate Conception
First Reading: Genesis 3:9-15, 20;
Second Reading: Ephesians 1:3-6, 11-12; Gospel: Luke 1:26-38

Reading through the gospels you may be surprised to discover that Our Lady is not mentioned all that often. She is present in the accounts of Jesus' early life and is there on the Hill of Calvary standing at the foot of the cross. Later on, she is with the apostles in the Upper Room, as they await the coming of the Holy Spirit. However, during the course of her son's public ministry, Mary slips into the shadows, becomes a silent background figure and is mentioned no more than a few times. One gets the impression that Mary must have been very pleased about this, that she never sought the limelight or wanted to be anyone of significance. In her book, what was of utmost importance was to focus attention on the son whom she brought into the world and cared for at every inch of his earthly journey. Mary always wanted to keep herself out of the spotlight in order to direct attention on her son.

The gospel describes one of the few occasions when the spotlight is well and truly focused on Mary. She is completely flabbergasted when the angel appears to her in a dream and greets her ever so graciously. We know that she is fearful at the greeting, 'Rejoice so highly favoured! The Lord is with you', because the angel Gabriel tells her not to be afraid. When God chooses a person it is a call to play a role in the life of his people. Mary's reaction to the message, that she is to become mother of the Saviour, is one of added confusion. In shock and consternation, at the magnitude of the request, she is completely dumbfounded and unable to utter a single word. Motherhood is far from her thoughts, as she is only recently betrothed to Joseph. And what would he think of her when she tells him about being the mother of Jesus? Although very religious, it never crosses her mind that she would be asked to become the mother of the Messiah. It would be quite a leap into the dark to say 'Yes' to this unusual and mysterious mission from God. Before she gives her definite consent she questions the angel as to how this can come about. Reassured that this is a request from God, Mary responds with that magnificent expression of love, trust and generosity: 'I am the handmaid of the Lord. Let what you have said be done to me.' Her response is total and her trust in God knows no bounds. Mary's is the most important decision ever taken by a human being. With this reply the wheels of salvation history are set in motion. Mary is prepared to make happen whatever it is that God wants of her.

This feast celebrates Mary who was favoured to carry God inside her body. God's plan to win back the human race into his friendship required that his Son should become one of us. The mission to be the mother of Jesus was given to Mary. To do so she had to be whiteness personified, fresh as a rose in her purity and strong as an oak tree in faith. God's grace reached into every dimension of her existence. As nothing unclean can enter the sight of God, Mary is free from all sin from the very beginning of her existence. Mary derives her gifted position from the absolute holiness of her Son. Wordsworth referred to her as 'Tainted nature's solitary boast.' She is in a class of her own, the only person who is utterly flawless and totally in harmony with her God. No one has ever more perfectly reflected the light of God than she does. She is all God would have a human being to be. All her life she is the delight of his heart. Mary is the one who, from all eternity, is chosen to receive spiritual blessings and to show forth the glory of God.

As we celebrate the beautiful origins of Mary, we get a glimpse of what God wishes for us all. His plan is to bring us back into the loving presence of his friendship. This feast demonstrates what is possible, when human life is touched by the grace of God. It holds out a promise that in the end we will all be changed by grace. In the meantime, we can learn from Mary how to be pleasing to God. The power that freed her from sin is at work within us, helping us to share in the glory of her Son. The greatest honour we can give Mary is to follow her example and centre our lives on Jesus.

Prayer of the Faithful

Mindful of the wonderful things the Almighty has done through Mary, we make our prayer for his special grace and protection.

1. We pray that our spiritual leaders may inspire us with lives that are holy and be truly servants of the Lord as was Mary.
Lord, hear us.

2. That all Christians may find in Mary a sign of hope and a source of consolation amidst the difficulties of life.
Lord, hear us.

3. We pray for mothers everywhere, that they may share in the blessings and graces of this wonderful feastday.
Lord, hear us.

4. We pray for the sick and the suffering, that the Lord may let his face shine generously on them.
Lord, hear us.

5. For our dead, that they may come to the fullness of peace in the feast of God's presence.
Lord, hear us.

God of timelessness and love, who, in the birth of Mary, has shown to the world the dawn of salvation, grant us a spirit of faith so that Christ may find a home in our hearts. We make our prayer through Christ, our Lord. Amen.

Feast of the Assumption of Mary

First Reading: Revelations 11:19, 12:1-6, 10;
Second Reading: 1 Cor 15:2-27; Gospel: Luke 1:39-56

The Feast of the Assumption is undoubtedly one of the festivals
of Our Lady which is most widely and devoutly celebrated in
Europe. Perhaps this is because it falls in holiday time, which
gives people the opportunity to gather at the great Marian
shrines. In France, the pilgrimages undertaken for this feast re-
call how their Gallic ancestors called upon the protection of
Mary and entrusted the good of the French nation to her as they
sought deliverance from war, famine and pestilence. They also
looked for her guidance as they faced an uncertain future. While
the Assumption is the oldest feast of Our Lady, we don't know
how it first came to be celebrated. Its origins are shrouded in the
mists of time. One of the earliest Marian memories is centred on
the Tomb of Mary close to Mount Zion where an early Christian
community lived. Pious belief has it that the apostles, on hearing
the news that Mary was dying, rushed to the scene as fast as
they could, only to find on arrival that she was already dead. On
opening the coffin to say their farewells they found it empty.
This feast is known in the Eastern Church as the Dormition or
the 'Falling Asleep of the Mother of God'. In the Middle Ages it
became the festival of Mary at harvest time because Mary reflected the life-giving, life-nurturing love of God. So we thank
God on this festival day for all our food and drink and for his
nurturing love in all its forms. The church celebrates the
Assumption of the Virgin Mary out of the belief that God specially
favoured Mary by taking her up body and soul into heaven.
Alone among human beings, she is with God, body and soul.
Mary is honoured in this way because she is the mother of God.
All her privileges flow from this. Since it was through her motherhood that Jesus was born into the world, it was fitting that the
flesh that had given life to God should not undergo corruption.
She was so closely united with the work of her son Jesus that it
was proper that she share completely in his triumph.

When we celebrate Mary as Queen of Heaven there is always
the danger that we might be tempted to overlook her humanity.

As well as walking the way of glory, Mary also knew the pathway of the cross. She lived through the harrowing events of the passion, standing by her son to the end and cradling his crucified body in her arms. Mary had to make this sorrowful journey in order to be part of the victory of the Risen Christ over death. The gospel story of the Visitation of Mary to her cousin Elizabeth shows her living the life of an ordinary woman and in no way different from her neighbours. Nothing could be more natural than Mary's desire to go and visit her elderly cousin Elizabeth who was expecting a child in her old age and who was very much in need of reassurance. The gospel pictures Mary racing through the hill country, carrying the news that she also is expecting a child – God's child. Hers was a humble, unspectacular life of faith, close to all of us in our joys and in our sorrows. Mary is of our own flesh and blood, the wife of Joseph the carpenter, who lived within the confines of the small village of Nazareth and hidden away from the public gaze. She was quite content with her lot and considered herself unworthy of special treatment. Yet it was to this ordinary girl that God gave the mission of bringing his Son into the world. From the cradle to the cross, her life on earth was closer to Our Lord's than that of anyone else. All that time Mary was the silent background figure, intimately involved in the drama of redemption.

Mary, assumed body and soul into heaven, is the first Christian who has finished the race that all of us have to run. She is an encouragement for us as we struggle on our pilgrim journey. Her Assumption is a reminder to us that the human story does not end in darkness, that there is another dimension to life and that death is not the final curtain nor does it have the final say. Mary's assumption body and soul into the presence of God is a joyful, happy event, not only for herself but also for all of us. Where Mary is now, is where God our Father wants us all to be. Where the mother of God has gone, the children are expected to follow.

Prayer of the Faithful

We make our prayer to the Father who reveals in Mary the glorious destiny in store for all who entrust themselves to his Son.

1. We pray that the leaders of the shurch and state, who hold authority and wield power, may show respect for those under their care, especially the poor, the suffering and the deprived.
   Lord, hear us.

2. That Christians may experience the love of Mary in their hearts and draw inspiration from her example of openness to receiving the Son of God into their lives.
   Lord, hear us.

3. For those who are shy and uncertain in human relationships: may the mother of God give them confidence and renewed belief in the blessings they bear.
   Lord, hear us.

4. We pray that the sick, the bereaved and the lonely may be comforted in their trials by the motherly concern of Mary.
   Lord, hear us.

5. We pray that our departed friends and relatives may be brought to the joy of everlasting life.
   Lord, hear us.

Lord God, you chose the Blessed Virgin Mary as the first fruits of the new creation. Hear the prayers we make on this joyful feast. May we follow Mary's example by sharing in her trusting faith in Jesus Christ who is the way, the truth and the life. Amen.

Mission Sunday
Gospel: Luke 24:46-53

Mission Sunday reminds us of the roots of our faith and the responsibility we have to keep that faith alive and to offer it to others. We remember the command of Jesus to go and make disciples of all the nations and we thank God for the faith of the first Christians who took that command to heart and put it into practice. We also reflect on our baptismal calling to be God's witnesses in our particular locality. The light of Christ that first shone in Galilee is meant to bring light to everyone who comes into the world. Luke's gospel stresses over and over again that the good news of God's favour is for everybody and no one is to be excluded. His gospel ends with the command that repentance and forgiveness of sins are to be preached to all nations. Our task as Christians is to make the gospel message alive and to advertise what God is doing in the world. At the same time we are aware that, in our lifetime, we accomplish only a tiny fraction of God's work. Nothing we do is complete and we are prophets of a future that is not our own. We lay foundations that can be built upon and produce end results that we may never see. One sows and another reaps but it is God who gives the increase.

Mission is about making the world a better place for peoples of all creeds and of all colours. Missionary activity involves the responsibility of reaching out to the poor and accepting the challenge, in the face of oppression, of being a voice for the voiceless and of taking a stand for justice and defending human rights. In our day there is a growing awareness that everyone has the right to their 'daily bread' and a right to what is necessary for life. Nevertheless, many live in conditions which are not in keeping with the dignity of a human person. We have only got to think of the areas of poverty and illiteracy that exist in third world countries, with the accompanying scarcity of housing and lack of health-care facilities. While the missionary church is involved on all of these fronts, her primary task lies elsewhere. Often those who have not heard the gospel are doubly poor, doubly hungry and doubly oppressed. While they are materially poor in lacking possessions, they are spiritually poor in lacking that hope which springs from the knowledge and love of Christ. Their hunger is not only for bread and rice but also for the word of God, which rekindles hope and gives meaning to their existence. We must share not just our bread with others; we must also share the Bread of Life. The specific contribution of the church consists essentially in offering people an opportunity not just to 'have more' but to 'be more' by awakening their conscience through the gospel. The true nature of the church as a universal family is to build a new world – a civilisation of love – where every human being will know and praise the one true God, be conscious of their dignity and live in harmony and peace with one another and the whole of creation. Mission Sunday provides the opportunity of focusing on the importance of praying for the success of the work that is going on in missionary territories. The sick are invited to offer their sufferings so that the people who are hungry for God will be fed.

While many of us admire the single-minded commitment of missionaries who work in the developing world, we are beginning to accept that, to be a missionary, one does not have to go to far-flung parts to enlighten the world. Nor do you have to carry the message out from a Christian land. Every Christian can and should be a missionary wherever they are. St Thérèse of Lisieux, who died at the tender age of 24, never left the convent grounds and yet God's love shone through her in such a way that she is known as Patroness of the Missions. We find the secret of her immense influence on the missions in the words: 'It is by prayer and sacrifice alone that we as Carmelites can be useful to the church.' If knowing Jesus is worthwhile for us, we should commit ourselves personally to making him known. We are a people on the move and are challenged to take risks by helping the needy and championing the cause of the poor. On this Mission Sunday we pray that the light of faith may keep burning brightly in the darkest corners of the world.

Prayer of the Faithful

Thankful for the gift of faith, we present our petitions to God the Father so that all the ends of the earth may find salvation in the name of Jesus Christ.

1. Let us pray for all in the church who preach and teach the gospel of Christ, that they may be empowered by the Holy Spirit to bring the light of Christ to all nations.
   Lord, hear us.

2. We pray for civic leaders and governments: that working together for peace and justice they may lead their people to love God and walk in his ways.
   Lord, hear us.

3. That missionaries may discover all the good there is in the hearts and minds of the people to whom they minister.
   Lord, hear us.

4. We pray for those whose generosity has aided the work of missionaries. May they experience the truth of Christ's words, 'It is more blessed to give than to receive.'
   Lord, hear us.

5. Let us remember our dead, especially our deceased missionary brothers and sisters, that they may rejoice in God's presence forever.
   Lord, hear us.

Heavenly Father, may the work of your church continue to make known the mystery of salvation and lead all people to eternal life with you, through Christ, our Lord. Amen.

Thematic Index